REASON OVER FAITH

ANTITHEISM & THE CASE AGAINST RELIGION

J. D. BRUCKER

FOREWORD BY JOEY LEE KIRKMAN

This book is dedicated to those who stand against all that is wicked in this world.

"Many people do simply awful things out of sincere religious belief...they believe that this is what God wants them to do, going all the way back to Abraham being willing to sacrifice Isaac because God told him to do that. Putting God ahead of humanity is a terrible thing."

Steven Weinberg

TABLE OF CONTENTS

ACKNOWLEDGEMENTS

Firstly, I'd like to thank Joey Lee Kirkman for agreeing to write the forward. He's a tremendously talented man who I'm proud to consider a dear friend. He tirelessly fights for the rights of others, who may not have the voice to speak out against the horrors of religious faith. Following his motto, we must *bully the bullies* if we want to make any progress. They must be well aware of our presence, to the point that we cannot be ignored. Joey is one of those people who the religious will fear, the freed will respect, and the fence-riders will listen to. Thank you again, my dear friend.

I'd like to thank my wife, who has supported me throughout my writing career. She has been terrifically supportive and I couldn't ask for a better life-partner. She's endured my endless tirades and late nights of writing, allowing me to finish this work in entirety. Thank you so much, my love.

I'd like to thank Dan Arel, Matthew O'Neil, and Joshua Kelly for the continued support throughout my journey. You three are wonderfully talented individuals and I look forward to seeing what the future holds for each of you. Thanks, my friends.

I'd like to thank Casper Rigsby, Armin Navabi, Michael Leamy, and the rest of the Atheist Republic team for the undying support. You all epitomize what this movement needs: passion, focus, and love. Keep up the wonderful work, ladies and gentlemen.

Lastly, I'd like to thank the skeptic and atheist community, for without all of your efforts, I wouldn't be writing this today. We all draw inspiration from one another, essentially planting the seeds of acceptance throughout societies worldwide. We must continue to work diligently if we wish to see those seeds sprout. I love you all, and keep fighting the good fight

FOREWORD

By Joey Lee Kirkman

There couldn't be a more relevant time than right now for *Reason over Faith: Antitheism and the Case against Religion*. As more and more of the world's population connect via the internet, more specifically social media, it is important that the people with an ability to reason have access to credible information. Imagine what our society would resemble if the average person solved problems reasoning from empirical evidence as opposed to emotion or hand-me-down beliefs. Even worse, reasoning from so called 'holy books' that are left open to interpretation by scholars, laymen, and sociopaths alike. Our political landscape is supposed to reflect who we are as a society. If we reason through issues before final decision-making, so follows our legislators and culture.

Why is reasoning necessary? In the context of this book, reasoning is to think. It is also an attempt to understand and ultimately form judgments by a process of using logic and accepting empirical evidence as a starting point. However, reasoning alone isn't enough. A person must make a conscious effort to be intellectually honest while contemplating issues in order to understand and learn. If something one thought were true, turns out to be false based on enough new evidence, a reasonable person would and should yield.

Why does reason trump faith? When there are thousands of denominations just within the Christian religion, each one claiming an ear to God, does it then stand to 'reason' that the differing sects are just making it up as they go along? Are the followers of the denomination really thinking things through? Alternatively, are they just that - followers? Is this really a good way to operate your own life? It certainly is not the best way to govern.

One denomination sees nothing in the scriptures that says we should shut the LGBTQI community out of the benefits of marriage. While another denomination reads scripture to say, it's righteous and/or a duty to stone them! Moreover, there are gradations along the continuum. There are Christian denominations that believe the LGBTQI community should settle for Civil Unions. Sorry, that is not equality. Furthermore, how did these religious groups obtain the power to vote on the rights of a minority in the first place?

If America legislated using reason over faith, the marriage equality debate would not even be an issue. In fact, it likely would not exist at all. These nasty ideas do not come about because a group of atheists decided one day it would be a great idea if we excluded people from their constitutional rights. These evil ideas came from one place, the Christian 'holy book'.

In summary, thousands of denominations exist within the Christian religion because so many people cannot agree on interpretations of the same manual. Therefore, it stands to reason that these differences wreak havoc on our political system. They are attempting to reason from emotion, and contradictory text and their personal ideology often won't allow compromise. In politics, this creates an extreme atmosphere of gridlock that can last decades. Imagine the work we could accomplish without religious dogma in politics! This brings us to the subtitle of J.D. Brucker's book, Antitheism and the Case against Religion.

I am often asked, "Isn't antitheism just the extreme counterculture to religion?" Not so fast. The definition of the word is not that black and white. One can hate the color green and find different shades of green pleasant. So first let's define the term because antitheists approach antitheism in a variety of ways.

"Antitheism is an active opposition to theism. The term has had a range of applications; in secular contexts, it typically refers to direct opposition to organized religion or the belief in any deity, while in a theistic context, it sometimes refers to opposition to a specific god or gods."[1]

Many Christians and Christian politicians all over the world assert a direct opposition to Islam. If you are one of them reading this, congratulations, you are an antitheist. Conversely, the same can be said about many Muslims and Muslim politicians worldwide that assert a direct opposition to Christianity or any other religion for that matter. With this in mind, on some level, it is safe to say that most adults are unknowingly antitheists.

Authors like J. D. Brucker and myself that choose to take the risk of labeling themselves an antitheist, often take a very nuanced approach. This impulse is almost always misunderstood. While we may view our Christian grandmother as a victim of religious indoctrination, we have no desire to picket her

---

[1] "Antitheism," http://en.wikipedia.org/wiki/Antitheism

church or show up on her doorstep to persuade her towards nonbelief.

Close to 100% of out-of-the-closet antitheists come from religious backgrounds. Is this a statistic one can fact check? I don't think so. Personally, I do accept the label 'antitheist' and every antitheist I've ever met came from a religious upbringing. We know how to differentiate between a sweet grandmother using her religion as a comfort blanket, and a crazy fundamentalist uncle who uses his religion as a weapon. For example the vote to constitutionally ban gay marriage as mentioned earlier.

The most poignant case for antitheism is at the political level. Time and time again, we see our elected officials holding up their particular brand of religion as their primary source of knowledge and morality. In a perfect world, I would like to see politicians running for office because they have a broad background of education and life experience. No politician can be such an erudite that he or she can become an expert on every issue. However, they are tasked with such expectations. They make decisions on health care, science, education, foreign affairs, tax law, medical issues and much more. Doesn't it then stand to reason that we should elect leaders because of their ability to make informed decisions, and not on the basis of how high they can hold their 'holy book'?

There are many brilliant Christians, and most of them are perfectly capable of governing. In fact, students from private Christian schools often test higher than their public counterparts. This is not about intellectual capabilities. Many progressive Christian politicians govern from a secular worldview and operate their personal lives from their religious worldview. Christian leaders like this help to create a foundation in which believers and nonbelievers coexist and progress is often achievable.

I think it is safe to say that antitheists practice anti-dogmatism. After all, this is our nuanced approach that is so misunderstood. Dogmatism, according to Dictionairy.com, is "...applying a principle or set of principles laid down by an authority as incontrovertibly true."[2] The Oxford Dictionary continues: "It serves as part of the primary basis of an ideology or belief system, and it cannot be changed or discarded without affecting the very system's paradigm or the ideology itself."[3]

As a former fundamentalist Christian, I can now speak openly and knowledgeably about what it means to have faith stifle and in some instances halt reasoning capabilities. I lived a portion of my life in the very ideological bubble I now take an active interest in opposing. My personality back then fit the dominionists' mold I now detest.

Author J. D. Brucker's examples in this book will make the case that reasoning from empirical evidence and not an emotion or plethora of denominational worldviews is not only good for society; it is good for the world.

[2] "Dogma," Dictionary.com,
http://dictionary.reference.com/browse/dogma
[3] Ed. John Bowker, "The Concise Oxford Dictionary of World Religions," Oxford University Press, 2000. Oxford Reference Online. Oxford University Press. York University.
http://www.oxfordreference.com.ezproxy.library.yorku.ca/views/ENTRY.h
tml?subview=Main&entry=t101.e2044

THE FREEDOM TO CRITICIZE

It's often said by those of faith that we secularists and atheists aren't free to criticize their beliefs simply because they are held so dearly. This idea, that religious beliefs ought to be held in a special place, is a terrible one. We should be free to criticize *all* beliefs. We should be open to hearing the arguments from the other position. We should be willing to change our minds and go where the evidences point. If we continue to allow the religious to dominate the intellectual landscape, our future as a species will be called into question. I agree that not all religious individuals are guilty of this, but we have seen what happens when the faithful extend their own brand of justice against those they consider apostates.

Last year, in 2014, we watched as Islamic fundamentalists ran from the headquarters of Charlie Hebdo as they shouted "God is great!" It was a time of great sadness not for just the French people, but for all of those who support the idea of free speech and the ability to mock and criticize ideas that which are demonstrably evil and wrong. What those men did that day will forever stand as a testament to why the freedom to criticize is so important. If they say, "Shut up about our religion, or we will kill you for it," a slight admission on their part is given. It seems as though the validity of their religions claims are not what's important; what's important is the strangle hold it has on society. I want to strip religion of this. The religious shall not dine on the weakness of the minority, for it is the minority that allows them to continue. That, in my eyes, can change.

We should push for change. We should empower the secularists, atheists, and agnostics. We should allow them to have a voice on all matters. If we can come together and have intellectual conversations and inspire rational thought, we must do so whenever we can. It's not always about whether or not a god exists; the future of humanity and the civil rights of other human beings is in question. Atheist Republic offers that platform; a place from which one can draw that inspiration. It's also a safe haven for those who cannot circumstantially be open and honest about their atheism and antitheism. I ask that you, religious or not, join in the discussion, allow your beliefs to be challenged and stand for humanity whenever the opportunity arises. The results will, I guarantee, please everyone.

Visit the *Atheist Republic* website at:

www.atheistrepublic.com

INTRODUCTION
THE MOST TERRIBLE IDEA

I am an agnostic atheist but preceding that I am a skeptic and a secular humanist; all of which are very central to my being. With those in the foreground, I've set a very clear path for myself. I cannot stand by and remain silent on issues regarding religion, secularism, and humanism. That being said, I must reaffirm my position on religious beliefs.

I care not what you believe. You're free to entertain any idea that may cross your mind. You may even form those ideas into beliefs; beliefs that may or may not correspond with the nature of reality. What I do care about is very simple: Human rights. Once those are infringed upon by the said beliefs, you've crossed a line.

The line is very simply drawn and easy to maintain only if one is willing to not cross it. This is perhaps why religion and humanism butt heads so often; the central core of religious belief is, in and of itself, a dehumanizing and ignorant proposition. Most religious beliefs maintain human beings are pawns in a game played on a scale much larger than we can imagine. As creations we are to adhere to the creator or creators without wavering. We have no rights outside that which the creator or creators handed down.

Religious beliefs strip us of our autonomy; the very thing that keeps us from becoming slaves of the slave masters. However, some wish to be pawns, tossed about and used as objects of joy and self-gratification on behalf of the creator or creators. As pawns, they'd also love to see you or I used as pawns as well and will sometimes cross that line in order to punish or segregate those who wish not to be pawns. This is why I wish to see institutions such as these, founded on primitive thought and motive, disappear from the public eye, leaving these pawns to play the game amongst their selves.

Religious beliefs have proven to be nothing more than wishful, and sometimes hateful, thinking. Why would I consider religious belief wishful and hateful? I can answer that concisely: The truth of a religious claim primarily depends on the existence of a supernatural entity, the pawn mover if you will, and since not a shred of evidence or persuasive arguments have been put forth in defense of this faith claim, the belief in its existence is entirely wishful.

How can religious beliefs foster hate? First, I must define what I mean by hate in this context. Using the standard definition, hate is an intense dislike for someone or something. We can freely hate people without remorse but my humanism won't allow for it. I hold no beliefs that require the degradation of another human being. I may speak toward the horrific nature of religious faith but I never claim to hate an individual for it. From my perspective, we're one single species among millions of other single species' living and dying as co-inhabitants of Earth. Certain religious beliefs, however, tell a much different story.

In Christian doctrine, there is a clear line between the Christian and the nonbeliever. One is righteous and the other is not. One has been given the gift of eternal life and the other has thrown it away. This can create an inhuman idea; giving the Christian believer the idea their lives are somehow more meaningful or appreciative than that of the atheist. This isn't limited to just Christianity; Judaism is guilty of this as well. While not as notable as Christianity's atrocities to humanity, Judaism maintains a number of guidelines limiting the extent of the human experience. This extends much further than that, as you will read later on.

Islam isn't without fault either. Fundamentalist Muslims often take a literal reading of the Koran. In that, they find the commands to commit acts of devastating violence. Infidels, in their eyes, are nothing more than miserable creatures deserving of death. We often hear that Islam is a religion of peace, but how in which peace comes is often left out; peace is the complete submission to Allah. With that, fundamentalist Muslims make it their mission to create a global theocracy and all those who do not submit to the word of Allah are enemies of Islam. I remember the day I watched Nick Berg suffer his tragic death as masked Islamic men shouted praises of God. I then suddenly realized something: Faith, when tied to ancient religious doctrine, provides us with only the ability to sideline our morals, compassion, humanity, and integrity.

What is Atheism?

Atheism, simply put, means the rejection of the "god" claim. I do not wish to speak for all atheists, so I will explain a bit why I am an atheist and what it means to be an atheist for me. I, for the longest time, sought God. I thought I had a relationship with him, Jesus, and the Holy Spirit. I prayed, attended church and Sunday school, read from the Bible, and I was even enrolled in a private Lutheran school for three years. I had deep, profound conversations with my peers regarding the subject, and I at one time believed Christianity was correct.

There was a catch, however; I had always been a little bit skeptical. There had always been that lingering question hovering in the background: What if I'm wrong? That was the question that eventually unhinged my faith. I was encouraged to "trust in the Lord" even if I had doubt; conveniently I was also taught to believe doubt is a part of my faith but never was I told unbelief was an option. So what was I supposed to do? Believe in Christianity even if I was unconvinced? That wasn't going to be an option for me.

I discontinued my faith as I began to slowly investigate religions globally and I eventually realized something in particular. Every single religion claimed divine truth, against all odds and all evidences. Christianity couldn't possibly be the right religion, with so many different religions existing all over the word, right? That question certainly didn't help my position. I finally cast Christianity aside when I realized two things: The core claims were drastically false and the idea of slavish worship was repulsive. Origin Sin, as the Bible describes, did not exist, there was no Adam and Eve, there was no Moses, there probably wasn't a Jesus, and Christianity developed slowly as almost every religion had once before. Does this sound like the one true religion? Does any religion, including their claims, stand out over another? I found the answer to be a resounding "no".

With so many questions, I found it unreasonable to believe in the tenants of any religion. I found it unreasonable to believe the god hypothesis held weight. That's what it really boils down to: What is reasonable and unreasonable to believe? If it had bad supporting evidence, it was unreasonable; if it had good supporting evidence, it was reasonable. As of right now, I find it completely unreasonable to believe religious claims. With that, I'm completely open to the possibility, but as of yet, I'm unconvinced and until I'm convinced I won't believe. Simply put, that's the extent of it.

Is Atheism a Religion?

It's been often said that atheism is a religion in the same way that all religions are categorized. However, those who believe that to be true are greatly mistaken. Atheism, as I previous described, is simply the rejection of religious beliefs. There is no deity, there is no dogma, there is no doctrine, there is no prophesy, there is no mythos, there is no heaven, there is no hades, there are no supernatural forces, and there are no requirements. How do we then define a religion? Merriam-Webster dictionary defines religion as:

"The service and worship of God or the supernatural, commitment or devotion to religious faith or observance, or a personal set or institutionalized system of religious attitudes, beliefs, and practices."[4]

Does it seem reasonable to conclude atheism is a religion? No, it doesn't. Those who claim that suggest

---

[4] "Religion," Merriam-Webster Dictionary, http://www.merriam-webster.com/dictionary/religion

atheism does in fact contain dogma, which is significantly untrue. Some atheists, I suppose, may feel that way, but there isn't a unifying conglomerate calling us to attach ourselves to it.

I feel this claim is also used to deflect from the arguments against religion. Have you ever watched a debate or read an engagement where in the atheist may claim religion is responsible for an immense amount of harm and cruelty? What does the theist often claim in return? They do not refute the claim; they posit atheism has harmed or killed far more. This is a slight admission on the part of the theist. They have no argument; religion has done a great deal of damage and their only way to argue against that is by erecting a strawman. That is intellectual dishonesty, in my opinion.

What is Antitheism?

Antitheism is the active protest to religious organizations of all different faiths; that is as simple as I can describe it. My humanism and atheism stands against all that religion teaches. I'm inspired by the atrocities done in the name of faith. I care for human beings; everyone, of all races, genders, and creeds. I do not wish to see harm done to others, particularly for silly reasons such as the religious obligation to do so, and this is how this book formally came to be.

Yes, there are plenty of things in this world that cause harm, shame, and death, but religion is where I focus my attention. Turn on the news any day or read any newspaper, you'll find the evidences I derive my antitheism from. Until religion ceases to teach bigotry, racism, "justifiable" murder, rape, genocide, slavery, and pure anti-intellectual dogma, I will continue to fight against all that I find wicked and ridiculous in a world dominated by religious faith and superstition. With that, I sincerely ask that you, the reader, consider joining me in doing so.

Can Atheists be Moral?

This is perhaps one of the most over-done questions still given today. It's quite clear that atheists can be moral, and can certainly justify so; though, I'm unsure justification is, in fact, required. If one wishes to engage in a discussion regarding the ill effects of organized religion and religious faith, their ability to know what's right and what's wrong is called into question; that we somehow cannot judge the violent and regressive actions of the faithful because we do not recognize a timeless, spiritual "judge". This is absurd. This is a non-sequitur and should be disregarded. Of course, this may not always be the case when engaging someone in debate. Many theists recognized the fact atheists can be moral, just as theists can be immoral.

Reason over Faith

This book will serve two separate arguments, both of which I feel desperately needs addressed in a single collection. I am against religious faiths of all kinds, not because I'm an atheist or I somehow "hate God" as others have quickly claimed. I'm against these faiths because I am a secular humanist and these faiths often violate the rights and experiences of my fellow human beings. As you read along, you'll find that I approach this question by exploring seven different conflicts that often erupt as faith exceeds its reasonable confines within the mind of the believing individual.

I will travel the depths of faith, examining the phenomenon of religious servitude and its effects worldwide in order to make my case. As I continue to make my way through this book, I'm reminded of my past. Though I was without a proper title, I would consider my recent past self as an apatheist; one who does not care one way or another whether a god exists or not. That even further extended to religious practices. I did not care what you did with your faith, just so long as it didn't bother me. I no longer hold those ideas dear to me since I've become a secular humanist. With that, I'll also present a case for humanism; how we can develop a positive society while religious influences and superstitions seem as prevalent as ever.

I will focus on the untainted mind of the child, those whom we will rely on in the future. Children are perhaps society's greatest assets; not in the sense that they are to be viewed as objects but if we wish to continue living in a civilized and coherent society, those who will come after us must have a nurtured intellect. Religious faith, as it has shown, stands in the way of that very idea. Not only are children suppressed in this aspect, I will identify the many ways children are robbed of their health and innocence as a result of the enforcement of religious commandments and pronouncements.

I will explore the role religion has played in the subjugation of women. In the United States, one may not expect the level of misogyny that still exists. In other countries throughout the globe, the case is far worse than anyone could ever imagine. Religious doctrine, including the Bible, Torah, and the Koran all depict woman as nothing but vessels; a lesser form of human with only one role to play in life: servitude. If these texts were not followed as ardently as they are today, even as ardently in the past, we may find ourselves living in a much better world.

I will examine the Islamic faith; more so, the growth of fundamentalist terror networks worldwide. From Reza Aslan to Glenn Greenwald, it's often said a number of terrorist groups find motivation for their atrocious acts of carnage not in scripture but in instances of military occupation or capitalism gone awry. Do those who support that idea have good reason to believe such to be true? I contend, they do not. I will detail a number of situations that clearly demonstrate why it is that Islam, as a religion, naturally breeds violent adherents.

I will expose the history of Christian fundamentalism. Today, of the total number of Christians, hardly any commit mass violence on a scale equal to that of Islamic terrorists. We're told Christianity is a religion of love, without scriptural mandates for violence; most keep to themselves without ever considering violent outings on behalf of their faith. But the past never stays quiet. While Christianity today is often wrapped in silver and gold, its history is stained with blood of those who held theologically-different beliefs.

I will detail the religiously motivated fight against science, both in the present and the past. The influence of religion, when on matters of science, is a terrible thing. Religious beliefs, particularly those from our ancient past, often conflict with what we've learned from science, even just in the past century or so. These often come to a head when dealing with matters involving children, public education, and state and federally funded organizations. Science helps us objectively answer questions regarding our past, present, and even sometimes our future; something of which religion has done nothing but hinder the progress.

I will explore LGBTQI communities worldwide, along with the fight for equality. Humans are humans, love and compassion should be freely expressed without religious impositions baring down. We all share a single planet, each of us with a very limited time on Earth. Yet, religious organizations today seem to believe they're doctrine over simple facts. With that, most feel compelled, as a result of their faith, to make sure others are forced to adhere to religiously-motivated moral pronouncements, whether they are actually moral or not. Equality among all humans is a wonderful thing and with that we can truly work toward a better society; that is, if religion is left on the back-burner.

Finally, I will present a case for humanism, tying together the arguments made throughout this book. Humanity is most important. Together, we can take the necessary steps in changing this world in order to make it a much more pleasant place to live. Religion inhibits many from experiencing life and as a secular humanist who was once religious, I can say that for certain. That bleak and muddy outlook on the world changes once the blinders are removed. It's much better to see the world in full spectrum rather than in black and white, because once we remove social lines, the "us versus them" mentality goes away. Once we leave behind superstition, fanciful thought regarding humanity, and hatred, we as a species can make amazing changes.

Summary

I hope to provoke thought in those who wish to change the world, and if you're finding yourself on the fence, I certainly invite you to join me and other secular humanists in doing what we can to make a difference. I alone cannot accomplish this task; this task requires the patience and diligence of those who wish to take it up. Think for yourself, for others, and for our future. Learn from the mistakes of those from the past and those still present with us. In the past few decades, we've seen changes of the likes we only wished were possible. It's often said religion brings comfort, community, purpose, and motivation. We must remember those are not exclusive the religious communities; where religion has proven to be beneficial, it has failed to standout as greater than any other community. Religion, faith, and superstition should be a thing of the past. Let's leave the childishness at the door and work together to build a better world

.

CHAPTER ONE
BLESSED ARE THE CHILDREN

Children are our most valuable assets as human beings. They hold the key to our survival as a species. They'll take care of us when we're old and frail. They will earn public government offices that will affect how governments world-wide operate. They will become policy-makers, bridging gaps between people and countries. They will invent goods that may extend lives, feed the hungry, provide water to the thirsty, and generally increase the human experience. They will develop cures for currently incurable illnesses. They will make discoveries on Earth, helping us understand our past so much more. They will travel the depths of space, providing knowledge of the universe and what may lie past its boundaries. How we raise these coming generations completely depend on those raising them.

I'm not a parent, so one may find some trouble with the direction I'm going in. I don't think it's necessary for me to hold an opinion on the importance of rational child-rearing; we as adults are a part of a co-operative society, plain and simple. We all have the responsibility to develop and maintain an enlightening environment for those to come. I care for children in the same way as I care for any other human being, but I think it's necessary to put much more of an emphasis on the development of children. Why wouldn't we do whatever we can to make sure every baby born

1

has every opportunity to experience a childhood free from dogma, superstition, and religious persecution?

Treatment of Children in Scripture

Children are given a very rough hand throughout most religious scriptures. A complete disregard of the cognitive development is very apparent, which is surprising if one wishes to believe these scriptures are of divine inspiration; a mind bestowing humanity with knowledge greater than what is achieved today. From a secular perspective, it's completely reasonable to assume ancient religious texts to have a very rough and black-and-white image of children in general; even relationships between the parent or parents and the child or children differ greatly from what we've come to understand today from those with the greatest of training.

In the Old Testament, these errors are made quite apparent. The very popular story of Lot and Sodom and Gomorra comes to mind. The story tells of two angels coming to Lot in order to save him from the coming demise of the city. When the rowdy townsfolk find the angels among Lot's family, they demand he turn them over for their sexual pleasure. Instead, Lot has a better idea. The text reads:

"Behold now, I have two daughters which have not known man; let me, I pray you, bring them out unto you, and do ye to them as is good in your eyes: only unto these men do nothing; for therefore came they under the shadow of my roof."[5]

---

[5] Genesis 19:8 KJV

Does this seem to be a loving thing on behalf of a father; would a mother willingly allow the father to trade their daughters for the life of a stranger? I suppose the humanist in all of us would stand against such a horrific notion.

Later in Genesis, we're introduced to Abraham and his son Isaac, whom God has plans for. He requires Abraham to offer Isaac as a burnt offering in order to demonstrate Abraham's devotion to him. As one would expect, Abraham obliges. The text reads:

"And Abraham rose up early in the morning, and saddled his ass, and took two of his young men with him, and Isaac his son, and clave the wood for the burnt offering, and rose up, and went unto the place of which God had told him. Then on the third day Abraham lifted up his eyes, and saw the place afar off. And Abraham said unto his young men, Abide ye here with the ass; and I and the lad will go yonder and worship, and come again to you. And Abraham took the wood of the burnt offering, and laid it upon Isaac his son; and he took the fire in his hand, and a knife; and they went both of them together. And Isaac spake unto Abraham his father, and said, My father: and he said, Here am I, my son. And he said, Behold the fire and the wood: but where is the lamb for a burnt offering? And Abraham said, My son, God will provide himself a lamb for a burnt offering: so they went both of them together. And they came to the place which God had told him of; and Abraham built an altar there, and laid the wood in order, and bound Isaac his son, and laid him on the altar upon the wood. And Abraham stretched forth his hand, and took the knife to slay his son. And the angel of the Lord called unto him out of heaven, and said, Abraham, Abraham: and he said, Here am I. And he said, Lay not thine hand upon the lad, neither do thou anything unto him: for now I know that thou fearest God, seeing thou hast not withheld thy son, thine only son from me."[6]

God is supposed to possess unlimited knowledge; would he not know Abraham's allegiance without this silly stunt? And this is supposed to be a virtuous act from which we can derive a moral lesson from? As a child, I was taught to believe Abraham was a man of great faith; faith great enough to allow a father to take the life of his son.

In Exodus, we find Moses attempting to convince the Pharaoh to release the Jewish slaves from captivity as mandated by God. Pharaoh does oblige after a number of plagues, but God internally convinces him otherwise. The text reads:

"And the LORD said unto Moses, When thou goest to return into Egypt, see that thou do all those wonders before Pharaoh, which I have put in thine hand: but I will harden his heart, that he shall not let the people go."[7]

As God said would happen, the Pharaoh refused. The final plague set to befall Egypt is a particularly nasty one, of which God intentionally sought to accomplish by forcing the Pharaoh to go against Moses' wishes. The text reads:

"And it came to pass, that at midnight the LORD smote all the firstborn in the land of Egypt, from the

---

[6] Genesis 22:3-12 KJV
[7] Exodus 4:21 KJV

firstborn of Pharaoh that sat on his throne unto the firstborn of the captive that was in the dungeon; and all the firstborn of cattle. And Pharaoh rose up in the night, he, and all his servants, and all the Egyptians; and there was a great cry in Egypt; for there was not a house where there was not one dead."[8]

God killed all of the first born children and livestock all throughout Egypt. This heinous act of blood-lust is revered among those within the Jewish and Christian religions, seen as an act of triumph for the Jewish people; I too remember feeling a sense of happiness as I read this in my early years. We were taught to have a sense of de-humanization against anyone who defies God's word, and that also includes children. This goes back to the phrase, "If they are not with us, they are against us." And the Bible truly embodies that notion.

That must certainly be the case for those who honestly read the book of Isaiah, where in which God lays violence on the city of Babylon. The text reads:

"Every one that is found shall be thrust through; and every one that is joined unto them shall fall by the sword. Their children also shall be dashed to pieces before their eyes; their houses shall be spoiled, and their wives ravished. Behold, I will stir up the Medes against them, which shall not regard silver; and as for gold, they shall not delight in it. Their bows also shall dash the young men to pieces; and they shall have no pity on the fruit of the womb; their eyes shall not spare children."[9]

---

[8] Exodus 12:29-30 KJV
[9] Isaiah 13:15-18 KJV

Later in Hosea, God decides to do away with Samaria for simply *worshipping* a different deity. The text reads:

"Samaria shall become desolate; for she hath rebelled against her God: they shall fall by the sword: their infants shall be dashed in pieces, and their women with child shall be ripped up."[10]

The killing of innocent children, the raping of innocent women; does this at all seem as though religious doctrine is humanistic at its core? Children are seen as mere objects, easily discarded without care or worry. Does this represent a society in which we should have? Regardless of whether God exists or not, these texts represent a culture of under-educated, ignorant minded people. And it's a wonderful thing there is no credibility to the truthfulness of these texts.

The Bible also hands out sets of rather unfair punishments regarding children. What are you to do with a rebellious child? In Exodus, the text reads:

"He that curseth his father, or his mother, shall surely be put to death."[11]

This punishment it elaborated in Deuteronomy. The text reads:

"If a man have a stubborn and rebellious son, which will not obey the voice of his father, or the voice of his mother, and that, when they have chastened him, will not hearken unto them: Then shall his father and his mother lay hold on him, and bring him out unto the elders of his city, and unto the gate of his place; And

---

[10] Hosea 13:16 KJV
[11] Exodus 21:17 KJV

they shall say unto the elders of his city, This our son is stubborn and rebellious, he will not obey our voice; he is a glutton, and a drunkard. And all the men of his city shall stone him with stones that he die: so shalt thou put evil away from among you; and all Israel shall hear, and fear."[12]

Is this a reasonable way to handle a child who rebels? God is seemingly incapable of properly addressing rude behavior in children; this is made well aware in 2 Kings. The text reads:

"And he went up from thence unto Bethel: and as he was going up by the way, there came forth little children out of the city, and mocked him, and said unto him, Go up, thou bald head; go up, thou bald head. And he turned back, and looked on them, and cursed them in the name of the Lord. And there came forth two she bears out of the wood, and tare forty and two children of them."[13]

We were all children once, rebellious in our own ways. We sometimes pushed boundaries, made mistakes, but we learned from them; never once would our parents have entertained the idea we ought to be killed simply for being as children are; after all, God created them that way, correct?

Religious Indoctrination

To state it plainly, indoctrination means to heavily influence someone into believing a particular set of ide-

---

[12] Deuteronomy 21:18-21 KJV
[13] 2 Kings 2:23-24 KJV

as, whether they are political, cultural, or religious. Most often, this is done when the individual is particularly young, when he or she lack the ability to reasonably conclude whether or not a statement is true. Those who've experienced heavy indoctrination may be unaware of competing theories, alternate hypotheses, or even whether the ideas hold any merit at all; those ideas are simply believed and held dear for an unknown period of time.

I'd never advocate for one to indoctrinate their child with strong atheist ideas either; I think it's very important that we teach children how to think, not what to think. I attended a religious institution as a young boy, around the age of 11 or 12. Up until that point, I will say, I wasn't too concerned with religious beliefs. I rarely attended church services with my family, occasionally took part in religious traditions, and prayed now and then; I was far from a firm believer and I don't think my parents ever were either. We were simply doing what everyone else was doing. That was, I think, the most important part of my experience as a child; I was never taught these things to be true by those whom I respected the most.

Since I was enrolled in this religious body, I do have firsthand knowledge regarding the practices of indoctrination. The pre-kindergarten class was heavily populated; the surrounding school district had a reputation of holding poor pre-kindergarten class, leaving this particular school the only option for many parents. We as older children often read them Bible stories, rehearsed prayers with them, taught them Christian hymns, and so on and so forth. What bothers me about it now was that I gladly took part in it. These poor children had no choice in the matter. They were being taught by their authorities that these particular sets of religious beliefs were true, without a chance of error.

And most of these children would stay in this particular school system, as most who had attended were my age. Almost all would tell you they knew God was real, Jesus walked on water, healed the sick, rose from the dead, was resurrected and ascended into heaven on the third day; to them, all of these things were as real as you or I. Never did they entertain the idea these things might not be true and neither were they influenced to challenge those beliefs. They weren't taught about other faiths and why other individuals find those to be true. It was a terrible environment for a child to have been brought up in and I sincerely hope I am not the only one to have escaped from the information they forced on everyone. I even refrained from challenging out of fear I'd be mocked or punished; in a way, I indoctrinated myself into thinking religious beliefs were off the table to debate.

So what age are children most vulnerable to indoctrination? Children are typically open to believing almost anything told to them, without question. During early childhood, children are most receptive which is why education is most important during this period of time. Learning comes faster, the memory is crisp, and children are generally open and willing to accept new information without inhibition. The age of reason is typically considered to be around 6 or 7, when the child begins to have the capabilities to weigh options and reach conclusions.[14] This is when we must be vigilant when trying to help them develop the *how to think* approach. The Socratic Method effectively helps the child develop the critical thinking skills

---

[14] Adele M. Brodkin, "The Age of Reason,"
http://www.scholastic.com/browse/article.jsp?id=7241 (July 1, 2006)

needed to maintain a healthy thought process.[15] This period of time hasn't gone unnoticed by those who seek to mold the mind of the young for religious reasons.

Most Christian church organizations heavily involve children in many different events. Sunday school, summer Bible camps, wilderness retreats, catechism or confirmation, plays, and musical ceremonies top that particular list. These organizations are quite aware how impressionable children are and it appears as though they're taking full advantage of that. Some evangelical Christian organizations fully and publically acknowledge what they're doing.

Known as the *4 to 14 Window Movement*, this global organization specializes in the indoctrination of children for churches willing to take part in the resources they offer. With their readily-available information, church leaders can effectively plant the seeds of faith before the seeds of doubt begin to grow sprouts. From their website, the mission statement goes as such:

"The 4/14 Window Movement is a global mission's movement. We help churches and families build strategy, community and resources for empowering the next generation of Christian leaders. Our goal is to support churches in every nation to Reach, Rescue, Root, and Release children into relationship with Jesus Christ and His ministry around the world."[16]

---

[15] Paul, R. and Elder, L. "The Socratic Method,"
http://www.criticalthinking.org/pages/socratic-teaching/606 (April 1997)
[16] 4-14 Window Movement, "Overview,"
http://4to14window.com/about/overview/

On their website, they advocate the instruction of religious dogma only so to solidify the child's future with Christ. I, like many prominent atheists today, have come to believe this form of intellectual mistreatment is child abuse; intellectually stunting the child's ability to reason rationally and convincingly.

Another organization, made famous among secular communities throughout the United States by journalist Katherine Stewart, is The Good News Club[17]. In 2012, Stewart released the book *The Good News Club: The Christian Right's Stealth Assault on America's Children*, in which she exposes the dishonesty on part of the Good News Club. The Good News Club, in short, is an afterschool program focusing on "moral development" based on biblical principles; this, of course, completely disrupting the line drawn between religion and government-funded organizations. The Child Evangelism Fellowship, the nonprofit organization behind the Good News club organization, has won a number of lawsuits throughout the past, giving them grounds to establish an array of child-centered biblical institutes set to turn innocent, honest children into soldiers for Christ. From their website, the focus of each Good News Club goes as such:

"Each club includes a clear presentation of the Gospel and an opportunity for children to trust the Lord Jesus as Savior. Every club also includes strong discipleship training to build character and strengthen moral and

[17] Child Evangelism Fellowship, "Good News Club," http://www.cefonline.com/index.php?option=com_content&view=category&id=13&Itemid=100049

spiritual growth. All children are encouraged to attend a local church."[18]

They believe they are doing something great; saving children from the torment of hell. They freely establish clubs throughout the world, using public school facilities after hours. They've been said to use games and treats in order to entice those who'd otherwise pay them no attention. If the word of Christ was as strong as those who claim it is, why must children be coaxed into believing it?

Since these sorts of clubs often take place after school hours, it's not unusual to find a number of children expressing what they've learned from the curriculum presented by the Good News Club. Katherine Stewart wrote in an article for *Santa Barbara Independent*[19] about the Good News Club and its effects on student-to-student interaction. In that, she tells the story of two children, one telling the other she was going to burn in hell for not following Jesus. While children are freely allowed to discuss their religious beliefs, I believe a line must be drawn, between simple theological attributes and outright fear-mongering. There is no reason why a child should believe they or their friends would or will burn in hell, and there is no reason why a child should develop irrational fear of something of myth and superstition.

In Islam, indoctrination is taken a bit more seriously. From a very early age, Muslims are taught to memorize the Koran; sometimes, this often holds im-

[18] Child Evangelism Fellowship, "Good News Club,"
http://www.cefonline.com/index.php?option=com_content&view=category&id=13&Itemid=100049
[19] Katherine Stewart, "Reading, Writing, and Original Sin,"
http://www.independent.com/news/2009/may/07/reading-writing-and-original-sin/ (May 7, 2009)

portance over studying other more earthly curriculums. This has two significant disadvantages. Firstly, this has a long lasting effect on the child's cognitive development, as it's primarily based on one particular source. Secondly, as a result of that, they will learn to reject other sources of knowledge simply because it deviates from what Islam teaches. This then, as I state previously, creates an "us" versus "them" frame of mind, completely carrying the Muslim believer further from enlightenment; never questioning and always accepting, brainwashing at its best. The very same can be said for most of the orthodox Jewish population. Anywhere religious instruction exists, expect indoctrination to take place.

Male Circumcision

Male circumcision is a common practice in most parts of the world, leading many to believe it's a necessity of medical nature and not of religious superstition. Yet, as the facts can be found, the opposite is true. It is a practice from our most primitive cultures, fueled then by religious hysteria and bolstered today by legend and myth. I had always known of circumcision as a religious tradition but because of its prevalent practice in western countries, I had always assumed it to have a substantial medical benefit; I was significantly, and unsurprisingly, wrong.

It's unclear as to when circumcision among males begun but it's believed to have begun in ancient Egypt. Stemming from ancient hieroglyphics depicting the practice there of, it's thought to have started during the 6th dynasty of Egypt; whether or not it was done so as a rite of passage, social status marker, or religious tradition is very unclear, but what's quite certain is what it has evolved into as the centuries progressed.

While exiled from Babylon, the Jewish people developed this practice as a cultural symbol of their faith. Several passages within the Old Testament explain this practice amongst Jewish people and the importance it held to those who scribed the books, bent on separating themselves from various other traditions during the time. It's first described in the book of Genesis when God formed covenant with Abraham, promising paradise to him and those whom come from his family line. The text reads:

"And when Abram was ninety years old and nine, the Lord appeared to Abram, and said unto him, I am the Almighty God; walk before me, and be thou perfect. And I will make my covenant between me and thee, and will multiply thee exceedingly. And Abram fell on his face: and God talked with him, saying, as for me, behold, my covenant is with thee, and thou shalt be a father of many nations. Neither shall thy name any more be called Abram, but thy name shall be Abraham; for a father of many nations have I made thee. And I will make thee exceeding fruitful, and I will make nations of thee, and kings shall come out of thee. And I will establish my covenant between me and thee and thy seed after thee in their generations for an everlasting covenant, to be a God unto thee, and to thy seed after thee. And I will give unto thee, and to thy seed after thee, the land wherein thou art a stranger, all the land of Canaan, for an everlasting possession; and I will be their God. And God said unto Abraham, Thou shalt keep my covenant therefore, thou, and thy seed after thee in their generations. This is my covenant, which ye shall keep, between me and you and thy seed after thee; Every man child among you shall be circumcised. And ye shall circumcise the flesh of your foreskin; and it shall be a token of the covenant betwixt me and you. And he that is eight days old shall be circumcised among you, every man child in your generations, he that is born in the house, or bought with money of any stranger, which is not of thy seed. He that is born in thy house, and he that is bought with thy money, must needs be circumcised: and my covenant shall be in your flesh for an everlasting covenant. And the uncircumcised man child whose flesh of his foreskin is not circumcised, that soul shall be cut off from his people; he hath broken my covenant."[20]

So it's quite clear: Jews are required, by biblical law, to be circumcised before they can partake in Jewish traditions. Moses, however, did away with the tradition until Joshua reinstated the practice. The text reads:

"At that time the Lord said unto Joshua, Make thee sharp knives, and circumcise again the children of Israel the second time. And Joshua made him sharp knives, and circumcised the children of Israel at the hill of the foreskins. And this is the cause why Joshua did circumcise: All the people that came out of Egypt, that were males, even all the men of war, died in the wilderness by the way, after they came out of Egypt. Now all the people that came out were circumcised: but all the people that were born in the wilderness by the way as they came forth out of Egypt, them they had not circumcised. For the children of Israel walked forty years in the wilderness, till all the people that

---

[20] Genesis 17:1-14 KJV

were men of war, which came out of Egypt, were consumed, because they obeyed not the voice of the Lord: unto whom the Lord sware that he would not shew them the land, which the Lord sware unto their fathers that he would give us, a land that floweth with milk and honey. And their children, whom he raised up in their stead, them Joshua circumcised: for they were uncircumcised, because they had not circumcised them by the way. And it came to pass, when they had done circumcising all the people that they abode in their places in the camp, till they were whole."[21]

The tradition carried on from Judaism to Christianity, though it was often interpreted as a spiritual circumcision since it was believed to resemble a sacrifice and commitment. Jesus, being the ultimate sacrifice, and faith, being the commitment, became sufficient for most Christians towards the end of the first century of the Common Era. However, the practice continued among Jewish Christians as they converted to Christianity.

Circumcision among the Muslim community is quite common, beginning when the religion found its footing. While Islamic texts do not obligate the circumcision of infant boys, it's strongly suggested based on the words of Mohammad, who required men in the Koran to follow the laws of Abraham. The text reads:

"Then We revealed to you, [O Muhammad], to follow the religion of Abraham, inclining toward truth; and he was not of those who associate with Allah."[22]

---

[21] Joshua 5:2-8 KJV
[22] Koran 16:123

As such, the laws are recommended to be observed, though there is no explicit instruction regarding the practice.

Circumcision is an ancient practice, derived from superstition and faith-based reasoning. Many argue the practice is a medical necessity; meaning, the boy is better off without the foreskin intact. But where does the actual science lie in regards to the operation? Many myths surround the procedure itself. It's commonly believed that the procedure is harmless with little complication, is endorsed by medical professionals, or the child will face a negative social stigma. I will admit I once believed these to be very true statements. But as I pointed out at the beginning of this section, they cannot be further from the truth.

Circumcision is a rather painful procedure and sometimes followed by medical complications. The foreskin is an extremely sensitive portion of the male body. With the heightened sensitivity, and the general act of cutting, makes the procedure excruciating for the one enduring it. With little to no health benefits concerning circumcision in general, this pain –while miniscule in time – still remains to be unnecessary and unavoidable. While if the procedure is done so by medical professionals, it's likely to be done so in a hygienic manner.

There is a tradition amongst the Jewish people, where in which a mohel[23], in an act of bloodletting, cuts the foreskin of the child and draws blood from the wound by creating suction with his mouth. This is not a common occurrence and only happens among extremely orthodox sects of Judaism which remain uncommon in the United States, but there is a growing concern regarding the transmission of sexual diseases.

---

[23] "Circumciser"

In 2012, the Centers for Disease Control and Prevention issued a recommendation advising against the practice.[24] This response came from the fact that two infants died as a result of an infection due to this religious tradition. In Israel, where the practice is quite common, a study found roughly 30% of those with herpes contracted the disease from this barbaric and, quite frankly, disgusting tradition.[25]

The procedure does not happen to be endorsed by medical professionals either. Though you may have the option to do so, and are often given the opportunity to choose, it's still entirely voluntary. A growing number of parents are choosing not to circumcise their child. In recent years, rates regarding circumcisions have dropped to almost 60% in western countries.[26] If a negative reaction comes to light, rational conversation between the parents and the child would be recommended concerning the matter. Without the necessity to circumcise, this leaves many to wonder: Was it worth it after all?

---

[24] Center for Disease Control and Prevention, "Neonatal Herpes Simplex Virus Infection Following Jewish Ritual Circumcisions that Included Direct Orogenital Suction — New York City, 2000–2011," http://www.cdc.gov/mmwr/preview/mmwrhtml/mm6122a2.htm (June 8, 2012)

[25] Amir Koren, Diana Tasher, Michael Stein, Orit Yossepowitch, and Eli Somekh, "Neonatal Herpes Simplex Virus Infections in Israel," http://failedmessiah.typepad.com/files/herpes-simplex-neonates-israel-7-cases-8-years-koren_nhsv_infections_israel_pid_2013.pdf (February 2013)

[26] Alexandra Sifferlin, "Explaining the Drop in Circumcision Rates," http://healthland.time.com/2013/08/22/explaining-the-drop-in-circumcision-rates/ (August 22, 2013)

Female Genital Mutilation

In many countries, female genital mutilation is thought to be a religious requirement by those who practice the act. It is typically carried out by older woman; much like the circumcision of a male, which is required to be carried out by men. While it occurs globally, the tradition is primarily found in countries with a high number of Muslim adherents, mostly in Africa but also in Malaysia and Indonesia as well. This despicable and horrific act often involves the removal of the female genitalia with a sharpened knife, for means to allow the poor woman to achieve sexual purity and remain moral in the eyes of her family and God. The girl is often between the age of 4 and 14, sometimes having the opening of her vagina sewn shut to, again, remain pure for her husband. It's also thought to be used as a means to decrease sexual pleasure during intercourse.

It must be said, even though religious bodies have denounced the practice of female genital mutilation globally, they're still religiously motivated incidents. In a report issued by Unite for Children, or UNICEF, they stated:

"Despite the fact that FGM/C predates the birth of Islam and Christianity and is not mandated by religious scriptures, the belief that it is a religious requirement contributes to the continuation of the practice in a number of settings. ...In certain settings FGM/C is widely held to be a religious obligation."[27]

---

[27] UNICEF, http://www.unicef.org/media/files/FGCM_Lo_res.pdf

It's often said by the faithful that religion and religious beliefs are not to blame for the vile and wicked acts done in its name; the people who commit the violence are guilty, and their misunderstanding of scripture and teachings are to blame. Still, I must say, the admission on part of those responsible for committing acts like this still associate these practices with their faith, and something must be said for that; religion breeds ignorance, which is ultimately the root of this problem.

Ayaan Hirsi Ali has spoken about her own experience as a former Muslim and victim of female genital mutilation. As a strong advocate for women's rights, she has written several books and speaks regularly on this topic. In 2013 she spoke with a journalist from the London Evening Standard and in that article she goes into great depth about the issue and the fight to end female genital mutilation. In the article, written by Alison Roberts, it states:

"Later Hirsi Ali says FGM is a symptom of the 'whole virginity obsession' within largely but not exclusively Muslim communities abroad, and sometimes here. Forced marriage, honor killings and child brides are similar horrors related to a 'purity' required in women but not men. 'Actually it should be a man's campaign. Why do they need a virgin? Why do they need a woman whose genitals have been demolished? Is that the only way to express their manhood?'"[28]

---

[28] Alison Roberts, "Ayaan Hirsi Ali: 'FGM was done to me at the age of five. Ten years later, even 20... I would not have testified against my parents,'" http://www.standard.co.uk/lifestyle/london-life/ayaan-hirsi-ali-fgm-was-done-to-me-at-the-age-of-five-ten-years-later-even-20-i-would-not-have-testified-against-my-parents-8534299.html (March 14, 2013)

By bringing awareness to this issue, by debunking religious claims, and helping young girls obtain the rights they deserve, female genital mutilation would be a thing of the past. Sadly, religious stupidity spreads faster than wild-fire; but we must not stop the fight regardless.

Child Marriage

Child marriages are prevalent in most of the world, including the United States on some occasions. Religious beliefs and the ideas of marriage often go hand-in-hand, allowing its adherents to marry young, sometimes prepubescent, women. According to the International Center for Research on Women, this is common. Their website states:

"No one religious affiliation was associated with child marriage, according to a 2007 ICRW study. Rather, a variety of religions are associated with child marriage in countries throughout the world."[29]

It's important to point out why laws regarding the age to marry are to be taken seriously. Most religious doctrines, such as in Judaism, Christianity, and Islam, teach against the conception of children before marriage. So, in order for those who follow those religions to bare children, marriage is required; if not, those who bare children before marriage often face social and judicial persecution and/or ridicule. So as a result, they are to marry, and sometimes far too early in age. Quite often, those young women who are married at a

---

[29] ICRW, "Child Marriage Facts and Figures," http://www.icrw.org/child-marriage-facts-and-figures

young age are either forced to by their parents or social group

Many of those involved in arranged child marriages are from areas of the world depleted in resources; parents in these countries often believe their child will be better off financially, there's monetary value in selling their daughter, or their child will be safe from sexual assault. With that, in an article for NPR, Jennifer Ludden wrote this:

"The United Nations Population Fund estimates that every year, more than 14 million adolescent and teen girls are married, almost always forced into the arrangement by their parents. The countries with the highest rates of child marriage are in sub-Saharan Africa, but those with the largest number of child brides are in South Asia."[30]

"Parents may offer a daughter's hand in the belief this will help protect her from a sexual assault that could leave her stigmatized in the community and unlikely to be married."[31]

Why would these parents feel permitted to do such a horrid thing with their own child? Religion and the economy, in most cases, can be to blame. So how do we draw out the underlying cause of child marriage? Culturally, we can examine the beliefs held by those who take part in this ghastly venture; or in the least,

[30] Jennifer Ludden, "Five Things You May Not Know About Child Marriage," http://www.npr.org/blogs/parallels/2013/12/01/247843225/5-things-you-may-not-know-about-child-marriage (December 1, 2013)
[31] Jennifer Ludden, "Five Things You May Not Know About Child Marriage," http://www.npr.org/blogs/parallels/2013/12/01/247843225/5-things-you-may-not-know-about-child-marriage (December 1, 2013)

claim their faith as a means to achieve the otherwise unachievable.

Living as a Muslim in a predominately Muslim nation, he can legally marry a young girl under Islamic law; sometimes as young as 10. This immediately calls into question the physical safety of the young girl. As I stated previously, if a girl is married, she is now allowed to conceive a child. Again, ICRW commented on this very subject. Their website states:

"Girls younger than 15 are five times more likely to die in childbirth than women in their 20s. Pregnancy is consistently among the leading causes of death for girls ages 15 to 19 worldwide...Child brides face a higher risk of contracting HIV because they often marry an older man with more sexual experience. Girls ages 15 – 19 are 2 to 6 times more likely to contract HIV than boys of the same age in sub-Saharan Africa."[32]

So what does religious scripture have to say regarding the marrying of children? For those who are allowed to marry, the Koran states:

"And those who no longer expect menstruation among your women - if you doubt, then their period is three months, and [also for] those who have not menstruated. And for those who are pregnant, their term is until they give birth. And whoever fears Allah - He will make for him of his matter ease."[33]

[32]ICRW, "Child Marriage Facts and Figures," http://www.icrw.org/child-marriage-facts-and-figures
[33] Koran 65:4

Along with this scripture, it's commonly believed that since Mohammad married Aisha. At the time of the marriage, Aisha was only 7 years old; it wasn't until she was 9 that the marriage was actually consummated. In 2009, Saudi cleric Sheikh Abdul Aziz Al-Sheikh stated:

"It is incorrect to say that it's not permitted to marry off girls who are 15 and younger...A girl aged 10 or 12 can be married. Those who think she's too young are wrong and they are being unfair to her."[34]

Because a 10 or 12 year old child wants to marry a man three-times as old as her? And if someone stops her, they'd be guilty of violating her civil rights? Of course, one can find those among the Muslim community who disagree, but again, it still stands: these despicable religious beliefs are often the reason why men find brides well under an appropriate age.

Let's not forget Mary, the mother of Jesus, was only 12 when she married Joseph, who is believed to have consummated the marriage between 13 and 14 years of age. The pedophile Warren Jeffs sits in a jail cell in Texas because he believed he was religiously allowed to marry and have sex with multiple girls under the age of 15.[35] The founder of Mormonism, Joseph Smith, had multiple wives under the age of 12.[36] Religious beliefs customarily allow the subjugation and mistreatment of those who are often too young to con-

[34] CNN, "Top Saudi cleric: OK for Young Girls to Wed"
http://www.cnn.com/2009/WORLD/meast/01/17/saudi.child.marriage/
(January 17, 2009)
[35] Biography, "Warren Jeffs," http://www.biography.com/people/warren-jeffs-20771031
[36] Troy, "Apologize This – Child Brides,"
http://www.exmormon.org/mormon/mormon216.htm (May 3, 2003)

sent to marriage, ask for help, or fight for themselves. While child marriages persist all throughout the globe for various different reason, it's wrong to ignore the role religion has played, and continues to play, in this important issue.

Catholic Church and the Pedophile Scandal

This is perhaps the most terrifying failure of a religious organization to date based on its lack of regard for the nature of the offenses committed. Maintaining an image of perfection was, and still possibly is, the sole motivating factor behind the Catholic Church and its efforts to cover up and harbor criminals. The Catholic Church often boasts about its generous giving and efforts to generally improve the lives of the sick, poor, and indefensible but the incidents involving pedophilia and the churches active involvement in keeping guilty priests from persecution completely derails any argument for good will the church has made.

They claim to be for the good of man but their actions have proven otherwise. They have systematically and effectively, allowed their priests to continue to hurt, rape, and mentally abuse the most innocent individuals on this planet. Parents are taught to trust priests and other clergy men; if a set of parents have been involved with the Catholic Church for much of their lives, why wouldn't they trust the man they've grown to know and love? Priesthood has become the perfect occupation for a pedophile and the church has become the perfect hunting ground for them.

A majority of these instances have occurred mostly in North America, but cases have surfaced all throughout Europe and Asia. In the United States, according to the Bishop Accountability website, a large number of priests have been involved in sexual crimes against children. The website states:

"The U.S. bishops have reported receiving allegations of abuse by 6,427 priests in 1950-2013, or 5.9% of the 109,694 U.S. priests active 1950-2002, according to the John Jay report. Including the 5,356 priests ordained since 2002 brings the total to 115,050, of whom 5.6% have been accused of abuse."[37]

Of these priests, how many children have been victimized? The website states:

"The U.S. bishops' report receiving allegations from 17,259 victims."[38]

The number is alarming and quite disturbing. Even though allegations began to surface in the late 70's and early 80's, it's quite reasonable to conclude these acts have been occurring for a longer period of time, extending far past the 1950's. If Catholic priests were simply abusing children by way of their position in the Church and community, that is where this argument ends. The problem has to with the church, as an organization, and its efforts to keep their priests from serving time for their crimes.

Civil lawsuits have been filed by families looking for moral and/or financial compensation for the trauma experienced by the child. The Bishop Accountability website states:

---

[37] Bishop Accountability, "At a Glance," http://www.bishop-accountability.org/AtAGlance/data.htm
[38] Bishop Accountability, "At a Glance," http://www.bishop-accountability.org/AtAGlance/data.htm

"Survivors often cite the prevention of future abuse and the protection of vulnerable children as key motivations and goals. The survivors of clergy abuse are painfully aware of these issues because often they were abused by a priest who had abused previously and was then transferred to an unsuspecting parish. Often a survivor's struggle to come to terms with the abuse is made more difficult by the way that a diocese or a religious order handled abuse claims."[39]

If criminal charges cannot be brought, it's reasonable for the victimized and the families there of to seek justice in any way possible, even if it's to expose those who are guilty. So how many cases were settled with monetary judgments? The Bishop Accountability website states:

"Over $3 billion in awards and settlements have been made comprising: $750 million in settlements 1950-2002 (partly overlaps next item)...$2 billion in large settlements and awards 1984-2008 with 3,547 survivors...$500 million in smaller settlements 2003-2008."[40]

With the willingness to monetarily settle these cases, it's apparent the organization as a whole has been quite aware of the litany of sex crimes reported. These are not crimes we can overlook with a simple disregard, as it appears the Catholic Church has done. If anyone internally cares for the safety and wellbeing of children, those who are set to care for them must be

---

[39] Bishop Accountability, "Settlements," http://www.bishop-accountability.org/settlements/
[40] Bishop Accountability, "At a Glance," http://www.bishop-accountability.org/AtAGlance/data.htm

kept under strict watch and accountability; this can be said for any organization that involves the care and nurture of little ones. This is a problem that demands our utmost attention and diligence. The Catholic Church, even as far as extending to the Vatican in Rome, is solely responsible for the crimes committed. These crimes stand as a testament to the focus of the church itself; The Catholic Church is more concerned with the safety and protection of their priests rather than the safety and protection of the children involved.

Summary

In short, religious organizations world-wide have caused a great deal of intellectual and physical harm to children, both in the past and present. We must all come to the understanding that those who are to inherit the world are most important, without question. It's our job to keep them safe, to keep them physically and emotionally healthy, and to help them develop a usable base for building knowledge. If we continue to allow them to be indoctrinated, mutilated, and abused, we shouldn't expect our species to continue progressing for much longer. We have to find the courage to stand against the wickedness that threatens our future as human beings. Religion, specifically organized religion, has, time and time again, proven to accomplish nothing but inhibit the future of many by stealing away a child's only chance at living a rational, intellectually-prosperous life; which is certainly something we must not put up with.

CHAPTER TWO
NOTHING BUT CHATTEL

Women have always struggled for equality and I think this is a very important issue that needs addressing. For much of history, women and their roles in society have always been governed by men, or collections of men, who felt superior to their gender counter-parts. Much of this misogyny I'm speaking of can be directly correlated to a religious view of women, drawing us to see that religion is most often the root of this issue. We've come to understand, far too long I'm afraid, that women are of equal value as men and deserve the same amount of respect and opportunity as men are given, anywhere on the face of this planet. This chapter will demonstrate how religion has played a critical role in creating misogynistic cultures world-wide.

Treatment of Women in Scripture

I was raised to respect women; that they are as able as men in every way, even if not given the opportunity. They are human beings, first and foremost. With that alone they shouldn't face inequality, yet they have. I've seen the society in America change even in the short amount of years I've lived. The fight for gender equality should be a thing of the past, but what hinders the fight is as sinister as the problem itself: religion. In scriptures throughout the world, in various different religions, women are constantly given the short end of the stick. If a particular set of people follow a religious doctrine that teaches the subjugation of women, as commanded by their god, is it surprising to see why it's been incredibly hard for women to earn respect globally? For me, the answer is no.

The Bible is a very male-driven collection of books; as you'll see as I make my way through the text. In the Old Testament, God doesn't wait long to express why it is that women are, in my opinion, viewed negatively straight from the beginning in the Abrahamic cultures. After God creates Adam, Eve, and the Garden of Eden, Eve is tempted by a serpent to eat from the Tree of the Knowledge of Good and Evil. In Genesis, it states:

"Unto the woman he said, I will greatly multiply thy sorrow and thy conception; in sorrow thou shalt bring forth children; and thy desire shall be to thy husband, and he shall rule over thee."[41]

So because she defied God, she was to experience pain in childbirth and remain a servant to her husband and answer only to him. Does the writer of Genesis have an equal idea of man and woman? Clearly, he does not. Even later on in Genesis, during the Noah story, the wording clearly indicates that a woman is clearly a man's property. In Genesis, it states:

"Of every clean beast thou shalt take to thee by sevens, the male and his female: and of beasts that are not clean by two, the male and his female."[42]

---

[41] Genesis 3:16 KJV
[42] Genesis 7:2 KJV

The male and *his* female? It's very clear to the reader what direction the book is going in. According to the authors, women are nothing but property and deserve to be treated as such. Even in the Ten Commandments, it states:

"Thou shalt not covet thy neighbour's house, thou shalt not covet thy neighbour's wife, nor his manservant, nor his maidservant, nor his ox, nor his ass, nor any thing that is thy neighbour's."[43]

A woman, specifically a man's wife, is viewed here as nothing more than property. Never is there a distinction between the possessions of a man and his wife; she is simply equal to his ox, ass, and house. Not long after, Moses gives instruction from God on the relationship between a man and his adult daughter. The text reads:

"And if a man sell his daughter to be a maidservant, she shall not go out as the menservants do. If she please not her master, who hath betrothed her to himself, then shall he let her be redeemed: to sell her unto a strange nation he shall have no power, seeing he hath dealt deceitfully with her. And if he have betrothed her unto his son, he shall deal with her after the manner of daughters. If he take him another wife; her food, her raiment, and her duty of marriage, shall he not diminish. And if he do not these three unto her, then shall she go out free without money."[44]

A man is free to sell his daughter into servitude and if she does not please her purchaser, she is to be sold

---

[43] Exodus 20:17 KJV
[44] Exodus 21:7-11 KJV

away to a land where her father has no control over her well-being. What about if an adult daughter is sexually taken without consent? The text reads:

"And if a man entice a maid that is not betrothed, and lie with her, he shall surely endow her to be his wife. If her father utterly refuse to give her unto him, he shall pay money according to the dowry of virgins."[45]

The poor woman is then forced to marry him? What exactly is the going rate for female virgins during the time of Moses? It's quite apparent, not even out of the second book of the Bible, that it's been written by un-cultured, unsophisticated, misogynistic men without any sort of progressively moral worldview.

Later, I will touch on the persecution of "witches" by superstitious Christian settlers in the early years of the United States, but the origin of those vicious crimes stem from one particular verse. In Exodus, it states:

"Thou shalt not suffer a witch to live."[46]

With this short but powerful writing, a large number of women died meaningless and preventable deaths. The book of Leviticus doesn't offer any goodness for women either.

Known as the law book of the Bible, Leviticus dishes out a vast number of silly, and quite frankly stupid, punishments for what are now seen as non-offenses; particularly, a set of guidelines on how to deal with a menstruating woman. The text reads:

---

[45] Exodus 22:16-17 KJV
[46] Exodus 22:18 KJV

"And if a woman have an issue, and her issue in her flesh be blood, she shall be put apart seven days: and whosoever toucheth her shall be unclean until the even. And every thing that she lieth upon in her separation shall be unclean: every thing also that she sitteth upon shall be unclean. And whosoever toucheth her bed shall wash his clothes, and bathe himself in water, and be unclean until the even. And whosoever toucheth any thing that she sat upon shall wash his clothes, and bathe himself in water, and be unclean until the even. And if it be on her bed, or on any thing whereon she sitteth, when he toucheth it, he shall be unclean until the even. And if any man lie with her at all, and her flowers be upon him, he shall be unclean seven days; and all the bed whereon he lieth shall be unclean. And if a woman have an issue of her blood many days out of the time of her separation, or if it run beyond the time of her separation; all the days of the issue of her uncleanness shall be as the days of her separation: she shall be unclean. Every bed whereon she lieth all the days of her issue shall be unto her as the bed of her separation: and whatsoever she sitteth upon shall be unclean, as the uncleanness of her separation. And whosoever toucheth those things shall be unclean, and shall wash his clothes, and bathe himself in water, and be unclean until the even. But if she be cleansed of her issue, then she shall number to herself seven days, and after that she shall be clean. And on the eighth day she shall take unto her two turtles, or two young pigeons, and bring them unto the priest, to the door of the tabernacle of the congregation. And the priest shall offer the one for a sin offering, and the other for a burnt offering; and the priest shall make an atonement for her before the LORD for the issue of her uncleanness."[47]

This shows a complete disregard of the female reproductive system; not to mention, a complete admission of ignorance on the part of the writers. If given by an all-knowing deity, wouldn't these texts prove a bit more helpful and uplifting, rather than degrading and ignorant? Setting aside debating whether or not a god exists, does it seem reasonable to revere a text in which it commands its readers to cast out a man and a woman to be banished if they have sex with each other while the woman is menstruating? I'm afraid it doesn't.

Toward the end of Leviticus, we come to find out how much a woman's life is actually worth. As you may not be surprised, a man's life is worth much more than a woman's. The text reads:

"And the LORD spake unto Moses, saying, Speak unto the children of Israel, and say unto them, When a man shall make a singular vow, the persons shall be for the LORD by thy estimation. And thy estimation shall be of the male from twenty years old even unto sixty years old, even thy estimation shall be fifty shekels of silver, after the shekel of the sanctuary. And if it be a female, then thy estimation shall be thirty shekels. And if it be from five years old even unto twenty years old, then thy estimation shall be of the male twenty shekels, and for the female ten shekels. And if it be from a month old even unto five years old, then thy estimation shall be of the male five shekels of silver, and for the female thy estimation shall be three shekels of silver. And if it be from sixty years old and

[47] Leviticus 15:19-30 KJV

above; if it be a male, then thy estimation shall be fifteen shekels, and for the female ten shekels."[48]

While a man's life isn't worth much, a woman's life is worth roughly fifty percent less than a man's; not to mention the extremely low value given for a newborn baby. Anyone with an ounce of self-respect, dignity, and even the slightest bit of humanity would find these texts appalling; not a single person's importance, not even including their existence, can be measured by values of money.

Deuteronomy doesn't do much better, I'm afraid to say. Two particularly vile portions come to mind, both of which regard the raping of innocent women. We understand how these traumatic events affect the ones involved. It may take years to get over the psychological harm caused, and in some cases the victims never get over it. It's an extremely personal, intimate, and terrifying experience, and those who perpetrate those crimes do not deserve an ounce of respect as a result of their actions. The text reads:

"If a damsel that is a virgin be betrothed unto an husband, and a man find her in the city, and lie with her; Then ye shall bring them both out unto the gate of that city, and ye shall stone them with stones that they die; the damsel, because she cried not, being in the city; and the man, because he hath humbled his neighbour's wife: so thou shalt put away evil from among you."[49]

"If a man find a damsel that is a virgin, which is not betrothed, and lay hold on her, and lie with her, and

---

[48] Leviticus 27:1-7 KJV
[49] Deuteronomy 22:23-24 KJV

they be found; Then the man that lay with her shall give unto the damsel's father fifty shekels of silver, and she shall be his wife; because he hath humbled her, he may not put her away all his days."[50]

These texts are barbaric, archaic, and unnecessary; serving to a culture during a time in which women were nothing but fodder for the wolves.

The New Testament, while largely viewed as an improvement, still lacks in humanity in some regards. Jesus and the writings of Paul were quite progressive for their time but by today's standards one cannot draw much from them. From Judaism to Christianity, much of the traditional laws were dropped, leaving a few to be followed. Jesus hardly spoke directly to his disciples about the treatment of women but Paul, however, offered a few tips to be followed. Before I present his remarks, we should understand how Paul actually views women. In Romans 1, the text reads:

"And likewise also the men, leaving the natural use of the woman, burned in their lust one toward another; men with men working that which is unseemly, and receiving in themselves that recompense of their error which was meet."[51]

What could Paul be referring to when he says *natural use of the woman*? This leaves one wondering how progressive Christianity really was in its earliest years. Paul keeps up with the misogyny, beginning in 1 Corinthians. The texts read:

---

[50] Deuteronomy 22:28-29 KJV
[51] Romans 1:27 KJV

36

"But I would have you know, that the head of every man is Christ; and the head of the woman is the man; and the head of Christ is God."[52]

"But every woman that prayeth or prophesieth with her head uncovered dishonoureth her head: for that is even all one as if she were shaven."[53]

"Let your women keep silence in the churches: for it is not permitted unto them to speak; but they are commanded to be under obedience as also saith the law. And if they will learn anything, let them ask their husbands at home: for it is a shame for women to speak in the church."[54]

According to Paul, as he deemed fit for Christian practices, women are to remain silent, remain covered while praying, and remain subordinate to her husband. The last point is then reaffirmed in 1 Timothy:

"Let the woman learn in silence with all subjection. But I suffer not a woman to teach, nor to usurp authority over the man, but to be in silence. For Adam was first formed, then Eve. And Adam was not deceived, but the woman being deceived was in the transgression. Notwithstanding she shall be saved in childbearing."[55]

Again, women are to be seen as inferior to men for simply committing the first sin of mankind; thankfully

---

[52] 1 Corinthians 11:3 KJV
[53] 1 Corinthians 11:5 KJV
[54] 1 Corinthians 14:34-36 KJV
[55] 1 Timothy 2:11-15 KJV

enough, we can say for certain there was no "first man" and "first woman".

Overall, Christian and Judaic scriptures do little to help the status of women. As a result, cultures world-wide apply these silly, archaic ideas, taking away the dignity, rights, and protection of women. Today, perhaps Islamic theocracies in the Middle East support the worst views of women, pulling inspiration from the Koran; a book no better than the Bible in regards to women's rights.

As part of the Koran, Surah[56] 4 describes how women are to be treated in Islam. The Koran, too, views women as objects in most cases; take for instance this text:

"And as for those who believe and do good works, We shall make them enter Gardens underneath which rivers flow - to dwell therein for ever; there for them are pure companions - and We shall make them enter plenteous shade."

Women are nothing more than rewards for living a good Muslim lifestyle. Also, men, much like in Christianity and Judaism, are to hold superiority over women on every occasion. The text reads:

"Men are in charge of women, because Allah hath made the one of them to excel the other, and because they spend of their property (for the support of women). So good women are the obedient, guarding in secret that which Allah hath guarded. As for those from whom ye fear rebellion, admonish them and banish them to beds apart, and scourge them. Then if they

---

[56] "Chapter"

obey you, seek not a way against them. Lo! Allah is ever High, Exalted, Great."[57]

Men are also allowed to marry multiple wives, including their slaves. The text reads:

"And if ye fear that ye will not deal fairly by the orphans, marry of the women, who seem good to you, two or three or four; and if ye fear that ye cannot do justice (to so many) then one (only) or (the captives) that your right hands possess. Thus it is more likely that ye will not do injustice."[58]

What happens when the wife, or wives, display lewd behavior? Though what exactly lewd means isn't addressed, the Koran tells the Muslim man how to treat her. The text reads:

"As for those of your women who are guilty of lewdness, call to witness four of you against them. And if they testify (to the truth of the allegation) then confine them to the houses until death take them or (until) Allah appoint for them a way (through new legislation)."[59]

If you have a slave wife, however, she is to receive a different punishment. The text reads:

"And whoso is not able to afford to marry free, believing women, let them marry from the believing maids whom your right hands possess. Allah knoweth best (concerning) your faith. Ye (proceed) one from anoth-

---

[57] Koran 4:34
[58] Koran 4:3
[59] Koran 4:15

er; so wed them by permission of their folk, and give unto them their portions in kindness, they being honest, not debauched nor of loose conduct. And if when they are honourably married they commit lewdness they shall incur the half of the punishment (prescribed) for free women (in that case). This is for him among you who feareth to commit sin. But to have patience would be better for you. Allah is Forgiving, Merciful."[60]

Merciful? Forgiving? Do these seem like commandments inspired by a merciful and forgiving god?

There is a very important reason why we refrain from unusual punishments today. We understand how the human mind works; the maltreatment of women on behalf of men in the past represents a fundamental misunderstanding of the nature of the human being. Today's mistreatment of women, however, is due to blindly following the teachings of ancient religious doctrines. If we wish to move past this sort of behavior, we must move past this sort of thinking. Why would anyone wish to agree with and follow misogynistic commandments? To please their god, of course.

Killing of Supposed Witches

The practice of magic dates back to humanity's earliest days, an idea quite prevalent throughout the ancient Near East during that period. The first mention of sorcery begins with the Code of Hammurabi, the world's oldest order of laws, predating the Bible by almost 300

---

[60] Koran 4:25

years. As for witchcraft and magic, the code of Hammurabi states:

"If a man charge a man with sorcery, and cannot prove it, he who is charged with sorcery shall go to the river, into the river he shall throw himself and if the river overcome him, his accuser shall take to himself his house (estate). If the river show that man to be innocent and he come forth unharmed, he who charged him with sorcery shall be put to death. He who threw himself into the river shall take to himself the house of his accuser."[61]

Though generally ignorant of the natural world, ancient people were relatively familiar with cause and effect. They identified that if something happened, something had to have caused the event to take place. This general idea, and the ignorance toward how the world actually operated, caused those of our past to draw false connections.

Today, the idea of witchcraft is relatively forgotten. Wicca, a modern dual-theistic pagan religion, is one of the few traditions of today that actively practice witchcraft, who consider it to be a form of the natural world yet to be recognized or characterized; a phrase I've heard used to explain things such as ghosts and auras. Throughout the most prevalent religions of today, most believe in forms of malevolent spirits, sometimes referred to as demons. These demons or evil spirits can be called upon and used for sinister purposes, opposing the benevolent acts of the god or gods for the purpose of pleasing the malevolent god or gods. These fanciful ideas were once ap-

---

[61] Code of Hammurabi, Code 2

plied more vigorously, resulting in the deaths of a countless number of innocent lives.

In Europe during the Middle Ages, the Catholic Church was very much involved with the persecution of women thought to be involved with sorcery involving the Devil. In the earlier years, however, it was very much discouraged among the people; it was relatively common to believe people were incapable of conjuring the "forces" thought to be used by those who accused people of witchcraft. The witch-hunt craze didn't swing into full-force until 1484 when Pope Innocent VII, who too had fallen prey to the growing hysteria, issued a papal bull[62] titled "Summis desiderantes affectibus" which formally recognized witchcraft as an egregious offense. The text states:

"It has recently come to our ears, not without great pain to us, that in some parts of upper Germany, as well as in the provinces, cities, territories, regions, and dioceses of Mainz, Köln, Trier, Salzburg, and Bremen, many persons of both sexes, heedless of their own salvation and forsaking the catholic faith, give themselves over to devils male and female, and by their incantations, charms, and conjuring's, and by other abominable superstitions and sortileges, offences, crimes, and misdeeds, ruin and cause to perish the offspring of women, the foal of animals, the products of the earth, the grapes of vines, and the fruits of trees, as well as men and women, cattle and flocks and herds and animals of every kind, vineyards also and orchards, meadows, pastures, harvests, grains and other fruits of the earth; that they afflict and torture with dire pains and anguish, both internal and external, these men, women, cattle, flocks, herds, and ani-

---

[62] A proclamation on behalf of an acting pope.

mals, and hinder men from begetting and women from conceiving, and prevent all consummation of marriage; that, moreover, they deny with sacrilegious lips the faith they received in holy baptism; and that, at the instigation of the enemy of mankind, they do not fear to commit and perpetrate many other abominable offences and crimes, at the risk of their own souls, to the insult of the divine majesty and to the pernicious example and scandal of multitudes."[63]

This would set into motion a terrible movement; one free of reason or simple rational thought.

As the hysteria grew, protestant churches felt the accusations were to be true. It was widely believed that a large number of women secretly and collectively formed pacts with the devil in order to cause chaos, death, and famine. Along with violating the first law of the Ten Commandments, you shall not have any other gods but God; those who were brought to trail and found guilty were to be put to death. Many of these trails took place in Europe during the 16th and 17th centuries, claiming the lives of more than 40,000 people, of which 70-85 percent were actually women.[64] The craze also spread to the colonies in North America.

Most are familiar with the Salem Witch Trials of the late 1600's. It began in Salem Village, when two young girls began hallucinating, convulsing, and speaking erratically. These girls, Betty Harris and Abigail Williams, eventually claimed they were under a spell cast by three women, Sarah Good, a slave named Tituba, and Sarah Osborne. It was believed by those of

---

[63] George L. Burr, "The Witch-Persecutions", 1896

[64] Robert Rapley, *A Case of Witchcraft: The Trail of Urbain Grandier*, (Montreal: Mcgill Queens University Press, 1998), pg. 99

the village the accused formed a pact with the Devil, taking part in satanic worship and demon-conjuring. This was perhaps brought on by the witch trials of the Massachusetts Bay Colony. In Massachusetts, children in Boston and Springfield accused women of placing spells on them. Eventually, the hysteria spread throughout the colonies in America. After the hysteria subsided, over 60 people were put to death, 75 percent of which were women.[65]

I watched a video a number of years ago where in which a few African women were bound by the hands and feet, doused in gasoline, and subsequently set on fire. These poor women howled, screamed, and thrashed about, doing what they could to try to survive. After some time went by, their lives were finished. As this happened, a mob of cheering men and women gathered around the women, taunting and ridiculing these helpless victims. They were subjected to this horrific form of death because they were found guilty of committing sorcery.

Incidents such as this still take place today, though not very prevalent. In some cases, governments have instated laws protecting the citizens from witchcraft by targeting those accused of being witches; countries such as Cameroon and others located in Sub-Saharan Africa are guilty of passing such laws. In 2009, eleven people were burned to death in Kenya as a result of superstition and religious fundamentalism. The referring article states:

"Kisii district residents confirmed the killings, saying an enraged crowd had gone house-to-house on Tues-

---

[65] Marc Carlson, "Historical Witches and Witchtrials in North America," http://www.personal.utulsa.edu/~marc-carlson/witchtrial/na.html (June 13, 2011)

day night, using a list of supposed witches in the region. 'They burned them alive in their homes,' one resident said, asking not to be named. About 30 houses were torched. Police drafted extra personnel into the area to prevent revenge attacks in a region already reeling from tribal killings during Kenya's post-election crisis. Traditional African beliefs, Christianity and Islam co-exist peacefully in Kenya. But there is widespread suspicion of sorcery, particularly in west Kenya, which has a long tradition of witch doctors and faith healers."[66]

I cannot say for certain, but I suspect these lives would have been spared if reason trumped the power of faith. We have to be vigilant if we wish to make changes. Yes, women are not being drug to the gallows regularly because they're considered witches but any action, direct or indirect, that aims to murder a human being based on faith-based assumptions still happens regularly and without remorse.

Honor Crimes

In 1989, a young woman by the name of Tina Isa was murdered by her father Zein, who was being investigated by the FBI for possibly taking part in a terrorist plot while living in the United States. While the FBI was listening to in-home surveillance devices, they accidently overheard the murder of the young woman. Her father and mother, named Maria, held the poor girl down as they plunged a knife six times into her chest. The referring article states:

---

[66] Wangui Kanina, "Mob burns to death 11 Kenyan 'witches'," http://www.reuters.com/article/2008/05/21/idUSL21301127 (May 21, 2008)

"Tina (her full name was Palestina) was the last daughter at home and the most American of the family. She had lived in Brazil, Puerto Rico and on the West Bank, but she was happiest in St. Louis. An honor student, she played high school soccer over her father's objections. Again over his objections, she went to the junior prom, only to be taken away by family members. On the night of her death, Tina's parents express anger on the tape that she was at work, then seem not to believe that she was at work at all. Then Tina's father says: 'Here, listen, my dear daughter, do you know that this is the last day. Tonight, you're going to die.' Tina responds: 'Huh?' Zein Isa replies: 'Do you know that you are going to die tonight?'"[67]

After she was confronted, her father murdered her as her mother mocked and jeered. She bled to death after sustaining wounds to her heart and lungs. Why was she murdered? Her western lifestyle shamed her family.

Many women throughout the world are subjected to horrific and painful deaths such as this for only dissatisfying the men in her family. Predominantly taking place in Muslim countries, women are killed for irrational, otherwise preventable, reasons. These women are sometimes murdered for wanting divorce, cheating on their spouse, being a lesbian, having been raped, and for not accepting an arranged marriage. Human Rights Watch defines this as such:

---

[67] "Terror and Death at Home Are Caught in F.B.I. Tape," The New York Times, http://www.nytimes.com/1991/10/28/us/terror-and-death-at-home-are-caught-in-fbi-tape.html (October 28, 1991)

"Honor crimes are acts of violence, usually murder, committed by male family members against female family members who are perceived to have brought dishonor upon the family. The marriage must make the choice to stay in the marriage and hope that the violence will end, or leave the marriage and hope that neither her husband nor any male relatives will kill her. A women who is raped, even if she can prove that she was a victim of sexual violence, may be killed by her husband, father, son, brother or cousin."[68]

Acts such as these have been condoned almost globally, but they still present a real-world problem for women living in fundamentalist households. They are expected to follow the word of the patriarch, most often the father or brother. They are told what to do and how to live, never given the chance to enjoy an existence worthy of living. These men are religiously motivated to maintain dominance, as it's instructed in most of the living ancient doctrines.

According to the Honour Based Violence Awareness Network, it is incredibly difficult to develop precise statistics regarding honor killings, as they are often carried out quietly in areas where crimes such as these are permissible. On average, 5,000 honor killings take place globally, with 2,000 of those coming from Pakistan and India.[69] In most cases, the woman aren't murdered but physically scarred for their crimes; many women have acid thrown on them, whipped, beaten, and sometimes cut as a punishment.

---

[68] "Item 12 - Integration of the human rights of women and the gender perspective: Violence Against Women and "Honor" Crimes." HRW, http://www.hrw.org/news/2001/04/05/item-12-integration-human-rights-women-and-gender-perspective-violence-against-women (April 6, 2001)
[69] "Statistics and Data," HBVAN, http://hbv-awareness.com/statistics-data/

This sort of barbarism is what we'd expect to see in a time dominated by the ignorant and narrow-minded. We live in a world that offers a variety of reasonable means to solutions. We can collectively come together and declare acts such as these to be a thing of the past. Women are human beings as well, deserving of as equality and acceptance as men. We shouldn't cling to the texts of our ancient predecessors; in fact, they should be cast aside, considered historical pieces, and replaced with a more reasonable, morally palpable definition of humanity and what it means to be human. Without the inclusion of violence towards women in its doctrines, religion, in this case, would be far less responsible. As for the time being, and as long as individuals continue to parade such texts with esteem, we'll continue to see honor killings and the mistreatment of women on a global scale.

Abortion and the American Christian Right

On August 19, 2012, Todd Akin appeared on KTVI-TV as part of his campaign. Abortion was a particularly hot topic during the 2012 elections, so it was to no surprise this topic was brought up by the news anchor. One particular aspect of the abortion debate revolves around rape and the right to end that pregnancy; an issue in which republicans flip-flop on. So, how did Akin address this issue? He said:

"Well you know, people always want to try to make that as one of those things, well how do you, how do you slice this particularly tough sort of ethical question. First of all, from what I understand from doctors, that's really rare. If it's a legitimate rape, the female body has ways to try to shut that whole thing down. But let's assume that maybe that didn't work or something. I think there should be some punishment, but the punishment ought to be on the rapist and not attacking the child."[70]

This demonstrates why I have a significant problem with certain people of power making decisions on subjects they clearly have no knowledge of. There is no such thing as a legitimate rape and there certainly isn't a biological mechanism that inhibits fertilization if the woman was forced upon by her male aggressor.

Much of the anti-abortion movement in the United States is made up of Christian-based organizations. Surprisingly, much of their motivation and discussion is based on biased and incorrect information; something I think those organizations should have a firm handle on. It's very common to appreciate the pregnancy of the woman and view the fetus that's developing within her womb to be a living human being. These thoughts and feelings are then projected when these organizations develop their strategies. From a secular perspective, the argument goes much deeper than that.

It's important to recognize what an abortion actually is and what types of abortion are in practice in the United States. We're all familiar with the posters, billboards, and picket signs brandishing grotesque images of dead fetuses, most of which appear to be well into the third trimester of the pregnancy. Among those who object to abortion, it's commonly believed these images correctly represent the majority of abor-

---

[70] "Jako Report: Full Interview with Todd Akin," Fox2Now, http://fox2now.com/2012/08/19/the-jaco-report-august-19-2012/ (August 19, 2012)

49

tions performed in America; at least, that is what is being portrayed by the use of the images during marches and picket events. These are grossly inaccurate.

In fact, most abortions take place before the 13th week of pregnancy. The CDC last ran an abortion review in 2011, in which they found:

"...most (64.5%) abortions were performed by ≤8 weeks' gestation, and nearly all (91.4%) were performed by ≤13 weeks' gestation. Few abortions (7.3%) were performed between 14–20 weeks' gestation or at ≥21 weeks' gestation (1.4%)."

So it's quite clear the majority of abortions are well within the first trimester; nothing close to the imagery used by those who oppose abortion. Late term abortions are relatively rare. Actually, there are only four practicing doctors in the United States who even perform third trimester abortion procedures to begin with.[71] With that, it's important to identify how an abortion it performed during each stage of pregnancy.

There is currently four different procedures physicians use when tackling this issue. If a woman in in the first trimester elects to have an abortion, there is a combination of surgical and medicinal means to achieving the abortion; these different procedures include the drug Mifepristone, the Manual Vacuum Aspiration, and the Aspiration. The drug Mifepristone is commonly referred to as the abortion pill, which simply introduces an abortion by inhibiting certain neces-

---

[71] Amanda Marcotte, "Meet the Last Four Doctors Who Perform Late Term Abortion in *After Tiller*," http://www.slate.com/blogs/xx_factor/2013/09/16/after_tiller_a_documentary_about_late_term_abortion_and_the_four_remaining.html (September 16, 2013)

sary hormones. The Manual Vacuum Aspiration, also known as MVA, simply removes the material within the uterus with little risk to the woman. An Aspiration, which may also be referred to as a D&C, happens when a physician dilates the cervix and manually scraps the contents of the uterus. The MVA and D&C are also used during second trimester abortions. As for the third trimester, the Dilation and Extraction is used. When this procedure is done, the fetus is terminated through an injection, the cervix is then chemically dilated, and the fetus is then removed manually.

So why is it so important that we secularists fight for the right to choose? Primarily, the objection to the practice of abortion revolves around religious convictions. Many prominent religious figures in America have contributed to the pro-life movement, helping us understand the religious motivation behind the campaign. In 2014, Pastor John Hagee said:

"When a nation embraces abortion, the death rate is greater than the birth rate, and so the nation is dying, because you're burying more people than are being born. And when you push Christianity out, that's what happens. And you people who are running around calling yourselves Christians supporting abortion, you are not!"[72]

Not only is he factually wrong, he's promoting the idea that you can't consider yourself a Christian if you support abortion. Those who are listening get the impression they should dump their supporting views on

---

[72] Hemant Mehta, "John Hagee and David Barton Claim You Can't Be True Christians if you Support LGBTQI Rights and Abortion," http://www.patheos.com/blogs/friendlyatheist/2014/08/07/john-hagee-and-david-barton-claim-you-cant-be-true-christians-if-you-support-LGBTQI-rights-and-abortion/ (August 7, 2014)

abortion if they wish to receive eternal life, which is demonstrably untrue, as some Christians do support abortion; just not the Hagee-Christians, I suppose.

The issue essentially boils down to rights: does the fetus have rights and if so, do those rights outweigh the rights of the mother? *Roe v. Wade* was a case heard by the United States Supreme Court in 1973, paving the way for the right to terminate a pregnancy. The Supreme Court ruled the 14th Amendment, as an extension under the right to privacy, did in fact cover a woman's ability to have an abortion. As for the decision, it allowed abortion in all American states, leaving third trimester abortions to be regulated on a state-to-state basis. Since, Christians have done what they can to maneuver around the decision.

One main objective of the Christian Right is to defund Planned Parenthood facilities. In January of 2013, Representative Diane Black (R-TN) proposed a bill titled *Title X Abortion Provider Prohibition Act.* In the Congressional Record, she stated:

"As a nurse for over 40 years, I have spent my career protecting life. As a Congresswoman, I am proud to continue this critical fight for life. With former Congressman Mike Pence's blessing, I have reintroduced his legislation, the Title X Abortion Provider Prohibition Act. This bill will ensure that no Federal funds are given to Planned Parenthood or any other organization that abuses their privileges as health care providers and fails to protect life. It is long past time for Congress to respect the will of the American people and to stop taxpayer-funded abortions, a heinous abuse of the law and destruction of innocent life. I urge my colleagues to stand up for life and to support this important legislation."[73]

While she did have an extensive career in the medical field, I find it hard to believe it's her only motivating factor. In her biography, it states:

"Black is driven by her Christian faith and an unwavering commitment to restore fiscal sanity in Washington, enact market-based health care reform, and return America to its founding principles of limited government and a strong free enterprise system."[74]

While only speculative, I cannot think that her faith didn't play a role in her actions regard the introduction of the bill.

Some believe congressional power can end abortion in America, others believe ridicule and violence can solve their issue. Protests and picketing events are completely permissible; we are completely allowed to express our speech freely. With that, those in the prolife movement are free to demonstrate. Hell, they can even yell "murderer" and "killer" as women walk freely into abortion clinics. While I acknowledge their right to do so, I completely disagree with their tactics; in the same way I would frown upon any atheist who would picket a Christian funeral, yelling, "There is no god!" There is a time and place, when we must be sensitive and when we mustn't be sensitive. These women are already making a tough decision

---

[73] "Congressional Record, United States of America, Proceedings and Debates of the 113th Congress, First Session," http://www.gpo.gov/fdsys/pkg/CREC-2013-01-14/pdf/CREC-2013-01-14-house.pdf (January 14, 2013)
[74] "Biography," U.S. Congressman Diane Black, https://black.house.gov/about-me/full-biography

regarding their pregnancy, why make it worse for them? Simply put, it's detestable and inhuman to treat another being in such a way, during a time that alone brings out emotional anguish.

Summary

If we wish to give ourselves the ability to transcend the moral compasses of those who lived anywhere from 5,000 to 2,000 years ago, we have to have the courage to fight against gender inequality. We are human; it isn't simply male and female. Religion has certainly contributed to the cultural misogyny that still exists today. We must drop the dogma that threatens to suppress nearly half of the world's population. Christopher Hitchens said it best:

"If you give women some control over the rate at which they reproduce, if you give them some say, take them off the animal cycle of reproduction to which nature and some doctrine—religious doctrine condemns them, and then if you'll throw in a handful of seeds perhaps and some credit, the floor of everything in that village, not just poverty, but education, health, and optimism will increase."

Imagine what this world would be like if we all were viewed as one in the same. I say, "What a world that would be."

CHAPTER THREE
IN THE NAME OF ALLAH

I sat in my school room, drudging my way through math class. It was a small school, only about 200 children in attendance. It was a small Lutheran school in the middle of small-town-America, if that puts things into perspective. I was a little over twelve years old at the time, things weren't so obvious to me then as they are now, which is why I failed to connect the dots on September 11th, 2001.

I was in a comfy spot; I believed God and Jesus were on my side, against the forces of evil that threatened our Christian way of living, or so as it was described to me at that time. I believe that was the first time I had ever heard anyone mention the word "terrorism" or "terrorist". I got the general idea of what the objective of 9/11 was, so as to attack a nation with precision and diligence. They were angry with us; *very angry* with us, in fact. I could understand anger then, but I failed to understand why they felt the need to bring down four passenger jets, three of which claiming the lives of more than just the pilots and passengers.

It wasn't until I was much older had I learned of the Koran and the tenants for violence; a terrible idea coated in a veil of peace. In this chapter, I will introduce the terrorist organizations and the wrath they have beset upon the world, all in the name of their religion. Far too often, I've seen those speak toward military occupation, oppression, and even capitalism to blame. I believe the issue is much simpler than that. I watched a video where in which a small boy, around 8, was shot in the head. Were his killers shouting their angst with American soldiers? No, they were shouting, "Allah is great"; a testament to the violent nature inspired by Islam and Islam only.

Mandate for Violence in Scripture

There are those that claim the Koran is a book of peace, promoting the spread of love and acceptance and tolerance. However, the contents of which call for Muslim adherents to wage war on behalf of their faith. If their faith is threatened, any means necessary to defend that faith is required. The Koran contains a vast number of commands, calling Muslims to both protect Islam from oppressors and spread Islam at any cost. The following passages have inspired war and the deaths of those who unknowingly became enemies with a religion that sought to dominate the world. From the Koran:

"Then fight in the cause of Allah, and know that Allah Heareth and knoweth all things."[75]

"The punishment of those who wage war against Allah and His messenger and strive to make mischief in the land is only this, that they should be murdered or crucified or their hands and their feet should be cut off on opposite sides or they should be imprisoned; this shall be as a disgrace for them in this world, and in the hereafter they shall have a grievous chastisement"[76]

---

[75] Koran 2:224
[76] Koran 5:33

"O Prophet! strive hard against the unbelievers and the hypocrites and be unyielding to them; and their abode is hell, and evil is the destination."[77]

"Therefore listen not to the Unbelievers, but strive against them with the utmost strenuousness, with the Koran."[78]

"If thou comest on them in the war, deal with them so as to strike fear in those who are behind them, that haply they may remember."[79]

"This because those who reject Allah follow vanities, while those who believe follow the Truth from their Lord: Thus does Allah set forth for men their lessons by similitudes. Therefore, when ye meet the Unbelievers (in fight), smite at their necks; At length, when ye have thoroughly subdued them, bind a bond firmly (on them): thereafter (is the time for) either generosity or ransom: Until the war lays down its burdens. Thus (are ye commanded): but if it had been Allah's Will, He could certainly have exacted retribution from them (Himself); but (He lets you fight) in order to test you, some with others. But those who are slain in the Way of Allah,- He will never let their deeds be lost."[80]

"O ye who believe! Shall I lead you to a bargain that will save you from a grievous Penalty? That ye believe in Allah and His Messenger, and that ye strive (your utmost) in the Cause of Allah, with your property and your persons: That will be best for you, if ye but knew!

---

[77] Koran 9:73
[78] Koran 25:52
[79] Koran 8:57
[80] Koran 47:3-4

He will forgive you your sins, and admit you to Gardens beneath which Rivers flow, and to beautiful mansions in Gardens of Eternity: that is indeed the Supreme Achievement."[81]

From the Hadith[82]:

"The Prophet passed by me at a place called Al-Abwa or Waddan, and was asked whether it was permissible to attack the pagan warriors at night with the probability of exposing their women and children to danger. The Prophet replied, 'They (i.e. women and children) are from them (i.e. pagans).' I also heard the Prophet saying, 'The institution of Hima is invalid except for Allah and His Apostle.'"[83]

"The Messenger of Allah said: I have been commanded to fight against people till they testify that there is no god but Allah, that Muhammad is the messenger of Allah."[84]

"The Messenger of Allah (may peace be upon him) said: 'One who died but did not fight in the way of Allah nor did he express any desire (or determination) for Jihad died the death of a hypocrite.'"[85]

This is only a small portion of the passages presented in the Koran and Muhammad's other writings. All together, these have the potential to create havoc and unrest for those who find themselves in the crosshairs of Muslim extremists.

---

[81] Koran 61:10-12
[82] Teachings and writings of Muhammad
[83] Bukhari 52:256
[84] Muslim 1:33
[85] Muslim 20:4696

Al-Qaeda

Perhaps the most familiar of all the Islamic terrorist groups to have existed is Al-Qaeda. It was established by a number of radical Muslims, particularly Osama bin Laden. During the late 80's, the group grew in numbers as a result of the war between Afghanistan and the Soviet Union. They've launch notable campaigns against many nations, particularly the United States and Yemen. Though they began as a force to protect Afghanistan from the Soviet threat, they're main objective remains such: To establish Islamic order throughout the world by any means necessary. Those they deem to be infidels are then targeted as opponents to their mission, also known as *Jihad*. Tom Quiggin writes:

"Jihad is war, according to al-Qaeda's perspective. It is an obligatory act for all Muslims. This obligation is described as being "fardh ain". Permission from parents or other relatives is not required if the jihadist is of an age of understanding. The aim of jihad is to achieve Muslim dominance over Daru Islam. Armed jihad is the highest form of jihad and should be undertaken against all enemies of Islam. This includes infidels, polytheists, as well as those who support them."[86]

The Merriam-Webster Dictionary defines an infidel as:

---

[86] Tom Quiggin, "Understanding al-Qaeda's Ideology for Counter-Narrative Work,"
http://www.terrorismanalysts.com/pt/index.php/pot/article/view/67/html
(2009)

"A person who does not believe in a religion that someone regards as the true religion."[87]

Without the religious context surrounding the motivation behind the acts of violence on behalf of Al-Qaeda, the organization itself would collapse; the men supporting the organization, as well as those who blindly follow the commands of their leaders, would find no purpose in attacking infidels if it was not for Islam and the Koran. Al-Qaeda has lost much of its support and leadership as a result of the death of bin Laden and other notable leaders, now only found in a small number of splinter groups throughout the eastern world.

The Taliban

The Taliban also found its beginning in Afghanistan during the war with the Soviet Union. After the Soviet forces withdrew from the area, the Taliban controlled most of Afghanistan. Mullah Muhammad Omar controlled much of the Taliban's territory, instituting sharia strictly. The referring article states:

"Most shocking to the West was the Taliban's treatment of women. When the Taliban took Kabul, they immediately forbade girls to go to school. Moreover, women were barred from working outside the home, precipitating a crisis in healthcare and education. Women were also prohibited from leaving their home without a male relative—those that did so risked be-

---

[87] "Infidel," Merriam-Webster Dictionary, http://www.merriam-webster.com/dictionary/infidel

ing beaten, even shot, by officers of the 'ministry for the protection of virtue and prevention of vice.' A woman caught wearing fingernail polish may have had her fingertips chopped off. All this, according to the Taliban, was to safeguard women and their honor."[88]

Again, this is what happens when uncultured, religiously-inspired men gain control of any given population.

The Taliban is only recognized as Afghanistan's official government body by three countries; Saudi Arabia, Pakistan, and the United Arab Emirates. Not only is the Taliban a terrorist group, they've been guilty of harboring other dangerous terrorists from prosecution, such as Osama Bin Laden. With that, they're as equally guilty as the dangerous perpetrators they protect.

I remember running across a news story while working my way through CNN's website. It nearly brought tears to my eyes; Taliban terrorists killed 132 children in an attack in Peshwar, Pakistan. I was simply at a loss for words. As I discuss similar topics later on in this chapter, I can't help but bring this ghastly and abominable attack to your attention because it perfectly outlines why I feel the way I do in regards to religion. Only faith, with the utmost conviction, seemingly grants one the ability to hold a rifle in their hands and end the life of an innocent child. And what did these men shout as they ran from the school building? The answer: "God is great!"

---

[88] Laura Hayes, Borgna Brunner, and Beth Rowen, "Who Are the Taliban?" http://www.infoplease.com/spot/taliban.html (2007)

Islamic State of Iraq and the Levant

The Islamic State of Iraq and the Levant, also known as ISIL, have been responsible for a number of human rights violations, mostly consisting of human trafficking, executions, and terrorist attacks. Apart from these crimes, they're also responsible for destroying ancient sites and artifacts, such as the Nineveh Wall, artifacts collected in the Mosul Museum, and the ancient city of Nimrud. ISIL is quite similar to Al-Qaeda in its origin and goals. The referring article states:

"ISIL Sunni extremists have long had a goal of trying to create an Islamic state, or caliphate, stretching across Iraq and Syria and possibly other parts of the Middle East."[89]

As a group, they're main intention is disturb cultures throughout the Middle East in order to establish chaos, giving them the chance to develop an Islamic theocracy. Even Abu Mohammad al-Adnani, the official spokesperson for ISIL, had this to say:

"If you can kill a disbelieving American or European — especially the spiteful and filthy French — or an Australian, or a Canadian, or any other disbeliever from the disbelievers waging war, including the citizens of the countries that entered into a coalition

---

[89] Amanda Scott, "ISIL's Agenda in Iraq"
http://www.voanews.com/content/iraqi-militants-conquer-territory-aim-for-borderless-caliphate/1940183.html (June 18, 2014)

against the Islamic State ... kill him in any manner or way however it may be."[90]

With convictions such as that, one can only speculate as to what extent this sort of speech can inspire death and mayhem. What makes ISIL much more dangerous are the ways in which they've seemingly mastered the art of recruiting. Aside from they're terrorist campaigns, they've launch a number of propaganda videos, calling the misguided to join their cause. They're also incredibly well-funded, gaining support from political bodies throughout the region, along with leeching money from those they attack as well as trafficking human beings, particularly women. While many of their actions are designed to instill fear and disrupt order, their religious intentions cannot be ignored or misconstrued.

Boko Haram

Recently, Boko Haram entered the news after committing a number of small terrorist attacks and kidnappings. Boko Haram is an Islamic fundamentalist group located throughout Africa, primarily Nigeria, Cameroon, and Niger. They are much like ISIL in that the organization, as a whole, seems bent on establishing an Islamic theocratic government throughout central Africa, with the entire world as a goal. In fact, just recently the group officially pledged an allegiance with the Islamic State of Iraq and the Levant. In 2012,

---

[90] "Stephen Harper condemns ISIS audio urging attacks on Canadians," http://www.cbc.ca/news/world/stephen-harper-condemns-isis-audio-urging-attacks-on-canadians-1.2773636 (September 12, 2014)

one of Boko Haram's former leaders, Abubakar Shekau, confidently stated:

"I enjoy killing anyone that God commands me to kill - the way I enjoy killing chickens and rams."[91]

While not as well funded and strong as ISIL, they also raid, pillage, and smuggle goods in order to fund their campaign; they're also heavily involved in human trafficking, as kidnappings top the list of violence they've created. With corrupt government running rampant throughout northern and central Africa, Boko Haram has had an easy time growing its territory; roughly 80,000 members strong, the group continues to develop quickly and efficiently. With the sympathy they feel toward ISIL, only time will tell how many more may continue to join those who seek to disrupt the progress of humanity, only for the faith they hold so dear.

World Trade Center, Tower One Bombing

In one of the first terrorist attacks perpetrated by Al-Qaeda, Ramzi Yousef masterminded the 1993 bombing of Tower One of the World Trade Center. Yousef, along with two co-conspirators, Mohammed Salameh and Mahmud Abouhalima, developed a large bomb which was then loaded into a van he had rented just before the attack. After being found guilty of the crime, Yousef stated:

---

[91] "Nigeria's Boko Haram leader Abubakar Shekau in profile," http://www.bbc.com/news/world-africa-18020349 (May 9, 2014)

"Yes, I am a terrorist and proud of it as long as it is against the U.S. government."[92]

Yousef was very much against Israel, one of America's allies. Yousef was a Muslim, afraid of, what he believed to be, the impending Zionist take-over of the Middle East. His religiously-inspired actions in 1993 led to the death of 6 individuals and a large number of injured civilians. He was sentenced to 240 years in prison.

USS Cole Bombing

In October of 2000, Al-Qaeda attacked the United States Naval ship USS Cole. While refueling the vessel in Aden, Yemen, USS Cole sustained a massive amount of damage which was caused by a large explosive aboard another ship. Eventually, it was made clear that Al-Qaeda was directly responsible to the terrorist attack that killed 17 individuals and injured more than 30 others. In a video obtained by CBS, Bin Laden wrote in a poem about the USS Cole:

"And in Aden, they charged and destroyed a destroyer that fearsome people fear, one that evokes horror when it docks and when it sails."[93]

Here, he clearly displayed his idea of the presence of the American military. Bin Laden's dogmatic vision of

---

[92] Peg Tyre, "'Proud terrorist' gets life for Trade Center bombing," http://www.cnn.com/US/9801/08/yousef.update/ (January 8, 1998)
[93] Rowenna Davis, "Osama bin Laden: The War in his Words," http://www.theguardian.com/world/2011/may/02/bin-laden-war-words-quotes (May 2, 2011)

the world only exasperated his hatred toward the western world and their support of the Jewish government in Israel.

Attacks on September 11ᵗʰ, 2001

On September 11ᵗʰ, 2001, 19 Al-Qaeda hijackers took control of four American passenger airliners. By nine o'clock in the morning, two of the airliners had already accomplished part of the goal; one airliners crashed into the upper levels of Tower One, while the other crashed into the upper levels of Tower Two. No less than an hour later, a third airliner crashed into the Pentagon. The fourth airliner never met its target; it crashed in rural Pennsylvania a little after ten o'clock in the morning. Black boxes recovered from the crash site revealed a struggle between the hijackers and the passengers which evidentially led to the airliner coming down. By the end of the attack, 2,997 people had lost their lives, making it the deadliest terrorist attack in history.

It was not evident who exactly was responsible for the attacks initially, but later it was revealed that bin Laden had orchestrated the attack. In a video obtained by the United States military, bin Laden is shown speaking clearly about his involvement. He said:

"We calculated that the floors that would be hit would be three or four floors. I was the most optimistic of them all... I was thinking that the fire from the gas in the plane would melt the iron structure of the building and collapse the area where the plane hit and all the floors above it only. This is all that we had hoped for...Immediately, we heard the news that a plane had hit the World Trade Center. We turned the radio station to the news from Washington. The news continued and no mention of the attack until the end. At the end of the newscast, they reported that a plane just hit the World Trade Center...After a little while, they announced that another plane had hit the World Trade Center."[94]

After the transcript was translated, it became evidentially clear bin Laden and Al-Qaeda were involved in the attack. Along with the attacks on Tower One of the World Trade Center in 1993 and the attack on USS Cole in 2000, bin Laden attacked the World Trade Center in 2001 as result of his religious convictions; in his eyes, the United States supported an Israeli takeover of the Middle East; an opponent in the eyes of bin Laden and Al-Qaeda. Osama bin Laden was eventually killed by US military forces in his home in Pakistan in 2011.

The Murder of Daniel Pearl

The incident involving Daniel Pearl broke the headlines when it was revealed that he had been kidnapped by Al-Qaeda in Pakistan in early 2002. As a journalist working for The Wall Street Journal, Daniel was in Pakistan after September 11th covering a range of stories. His abduction took place as he believed to have been on his way to interview Sheikh Mubarak Ali Gilani but his travel was interrupted when Al-Qaeda members seized him with force.

---

[94] "Transcript of Usama bin Laden Video Tape"
http://www.defense.gov/news/Dec2001/d20011213ubl.pdf (December 2001)

While in captivity, Al-Qaeda members attempted to barter with the US military; they claimed to offer Daniel in exchange for the release of a number of detained terrorists. When their demands were not met, his captors placed him in front of an operating camera. Before his pending demise, he chillingly stated:

"My name is Daniel Pearl. I am a Jewish American from Encino, California USA. I come from, uh, on my father's side the family is Zionist. My father's Jewish, my mother's Jewish, I'm Jewish. My family follows Judaism. We've made numerous family visits to Israel. Back in the town of Bnei Brak there is a street named after my great grandfather Chaim Pearl who is one of the founders of the town."[95]

Afterward, his head was brutally removed from the shoulders. His body was then taken to the city from which he was kidnapped, Karachi, Pakistan, and buried in a shallow grave. This event led to media outlets in the United States extensively covering future murders on behalf of Al-Qaeda. What could convince someone, who may have been an otherwise intelligent and intellectual being, to hold another human being down and for several minutes and attempt to severe the head from the shoulders? It's a terrible thing such a question must be internally asked by anyone. Daniel Pearl, and others who met the same fate as him, may still be alive if not for the religious convictions held by those who operated Al-Qaeda.

Madrid Train Bombings

In March of 2004, Islamic fundamentalists attacked the train system in Madrid, Spain. In the coordinated attack, several bombs were detonated throughout Madrid, resulting in the deaths of 191 people, making it the most deadly terrorist in Spain's history. What made this attack particularly interesting was the attackers; they had not a single tie to the network of terrorists belonging to Al-Qaeda, but it was later found that they shared the same ideology belonging to those who call themselves members.

191 people lost their lives that day because a number of independent Islamic fundamentalists only sympathized with the efforts of Al-Qaeda. They had believed there existed a centralized "war on Islam" from which they felt the need to defend their faith. With the United States war with Iraq, they ignored the motivation behind the US government's involvements; instead, they simply saw the western world encroaching on an area that remained predominantly Muslim for such a long time. While the occupation of Iraq upset and enraged the Madrid terrorists, their faith is what spurred that attacks. Without the convictions held by those who perpetrated the attack, I question whether these men would have the extreme dedication it took to place a number of homemade bombs throughout Madrid.

The Murder of James Foley and Joel Sotloff

James Foley worked as a journalist for most of his life. When he was kidnapped, he was visiting Syria while working on a film with John Cantile; he and Cantile were taken by a group of soldiers. It was believed, for most of his captivity, he had been held in Damascus as a prisoner of the Syrian government. It was later revealed he was being held captive by ISIL.

A farewell letter from Foley was eventually sent to his family. In it, he spoke fondly of his family and friends, bidding them farewell in a gracious way. I remember reading the letter when it was published by The Washington Post; it was certainly emotionally wrenching to read the last written words of a man who dedicated his life to making the world a better place. In a video released by ISIL, it was revealed that Foley had been beheaded by the now infamous Jihadi John; in the video, Jihadi John expressed disgust toward the US government and the bombings in Iraq. Afterward, Jihadi John proceeded to murder Foley in a brutal fashion.

Jihadi John was also the murderer of Joel Sotloff. Sotloff was a journalist working in Turkey and Syria when he was kidnapped. In the beheading video released by ISIL, Jihadi John stated:

"I'm back, Obama, and I'm back because of your arrogant foreign policy towards the Islamic State, because of your insistence on continuing your bombings and on Mosul Dam, despite our serious warnings. So just as your missiles continue to strike our people, our knife will continue to strike the necks of your people."[96]

---

[96] Chelsea Carter and Ashley Fantz, "ISIS video shows beheading of American journalist Steven Sotloff," http://www.cnn.com/2014/09/02/world/meast/isis-american-journalist-sotloff/ (September 9, 2014)

Is this a rational means to addressing an issue? Meeting violence with violence has never proved to end violence. Men like Jihadi John and those who follow similar tenants will continue to assault and kill those who oppose their faith until the ideas surrounding the said faith are extinguished. ISIL believes they are righteous in their actions because the Koran teaches so. The Koran does not teach tolerance; on the contrary, it teaches ignorance and intolerance. They kidnap men and women who they believe to be significant to the enemies of their faith, which is directly taken from the Koran. There exists not a shred of reason, humanism, and love; there is only hate, anger, and faith.

ISIL Suicide Bombings

ISIL has launched numerous suicide bombing campaigns throughout its short history. It's commonly understood that these suicide bombers believe they are doing right by Allah; they are, in their minds, solidifying a spot in heaven for pleasing their lord. Faith is an incredibly powerful force within the mind. For someone, who seems to be completely cognitively aware of their actions, to attach an explosive device to their bodies and detonate the said device amongst a swarm of other human beings must indeed by an incredible feat. However, if you feel as though your god, who you believe created you, gave you purpose and a place in paradise, commands you to do such a terrible thing, then it's conceivably appropriate to expect someone to do such a thing.

We quite frequently bear witness to devastating and destructive attacks, often resulting in the loss of a countless number of lives. As I'm writing this, 33 innocent lives were lost in Afghanistan as an ISIL suicide bomber detonated an explosive device attached to a motorcycle in the city of Jalalabad.[97] In late March of 2015, ISIL killed 15 soldiers at a military check point in Lybia.[98] Earlier in that same month, an Australian teenager died in a suicide attack in Iraq.[99] "From Australia?" you may ask. This is why these ideas are so dangerous.

They claim the lives of more than just the attacker's targets; they claim the lives of the suicide bombers as well. Some may say, "Good riddance" about those who planned the attack, but I do not sympathize with their position. For me, I see the bomber as a victim as well; a victim of their faith. They are, seemingly, unaware of the power of faith. Some who believe in a god may mistake this as the presence of the being they worship. They feel strong in regards to their religious convictions because they've allowed faith to make itself at home. It's a sad and humbling thing to think about.

[97] Lydia Gress, "At least 33 killed in suicide bomb attack by Islamic State on bank in eastern Afghan city," http://www.dailymail.co.uk/news/article-3044582/At-30-killed-suicide-bomb-attack-bank-eastern-Afghan-city.html#ixzz3XhMosj40 (April 18, 2014)

[98] "ISIL claims suicide attack in Libya's Benghazi," http://www.aljazeera.com/news/middleeast/2015/03/isil-claims-suicide-attack-libya-benghazi-150325011007654.html (March 25, 2015)

[99] Michael Safi, "Exclusive: blog shows Australian teen reported dead in Iraq suicide attack had planned bombings in Melbourne" http://www.theguardian.com/world/2015/mar/12/exclusive-blog-shows-australian-teen-reported-dead-in-iraq-suicide-attack-had-planned-bombings-in-melbourne (March 11, 2015)

The Albu Nimr Massacre

This terribly tragic incident occurred throughout October and November of 2014. The Albu Nimr tribe is a collection of Sunni Muslims who sided with the Iraqi government in regards to the coalition to bring ISIL to an end. In doing so, ISIL ignorantly made them a target. As I stated previously, ISIL believes anyone who thinks, in theological terms, differently than them ought to be killed; apostates, ISIL calls them.

Since the end of 2014, ISIL has killed well over 400 people belonging to the Albu Nimr tribe; some also include children and pregnant women. *Pregnant women.* This is the type of behavior that results from religious convictions; these innocent people lost their lives simply because other people didn't think they were "holy and righteous" enough. I long for the day I no longer read headlines breaking the story on dismal instances such as this.

Mass-Beheading of Egyptian Christians

The video showed twenty-one men, dressed in orange jump suits stood on a Libyan beach, each with a man dressed in black standing behind them. The apparent leader, during the lengthy diatribe, stated:

"The sea you have hidden Sheikh Osama bin Laden's body in, we swear to Allah, we will mix it with your blood."[100]

After the heated speech, he then commanded the men dressed in black to commence with the mission; each of the twenty-one men was then beheaded. This was a video released by ISIL in February of 2015. These men were Coptic Christians from Egypt, captured during two different instances of warfare involving ISIL. These men had done nothing wrong; they were only guilty of being born in a country who defied ISIL's theological ideologies. Brutality, savagery, and stupidity do not even begin to describe the actions perpetrated by those belonging to ISIL. To be quite honest, words escape me. I've poured over dozens of instances of violence and death, leaving me much more enraged than I had ever imagined. It's a terrible, terrible thing such a motive even exists.

The Destruction of Nimrud

ISIL not only commits acts of violence to inspire fear in those they target, they are also dedicated to the desecration of ancient historical sites, particularly sites that which hold a theological significance to those they oppose. In this case, Nimrud was the target of ISIL. Nimrud was a city built by Assyrians around the 13th century of the Common Era. Having only been excavated roughly sixty years ago, it was an important site to the history of Iraq and those of the past. To

---

[100] CNN Staff, "ISIS video appears to show beheadings of Egyptian Coptic Christians in Libya," http://www.cnn.com/2015/02/15/middleeast/isis-video-beheadings-christians/ (February 15, 2015)

those of ISIL, however, Nimrud only represented blasphemy; that with which does not correspond with their faith.

I studied history while I attended college, which had always been a very interesting and stimulating subject for me. I appreciate the history of our past, and the advancements we've made since our early history only confirms more and more that the innovativeness of our ancestors ought not to be forgotten. To those who dogmatically choose faith over reason, these sites are culturally meaningless, worthy of nothing but destruction. What's the best way to maintain an ignorant population? It's done so by removing anything that which holds cultural significance; faith, once again, in practice.

The Mass Kidnapping of Schoolgirls

On April 15th, 2014, the Islamic group attacked a school in the Nigerian town of Chibok. The attack ended with the abduction of over 300 young girls who were, at that time, present during the time of the attack. Not much was known about the whereabouts of the abducted girls, as well as those who had perpetrated this horrific crime. It was later revealed Boko Haram was responsible. In a video released by Boko Haram, Abubakar Shekau stated:

"I abducted your girls. I will sell them in the market, by Allah…There is a market for selling humans. Allah says I should sell. He commands me to sell. I will sell women. I sell women."[101]

---

[101] Aminu Abubakar and Josh Levs, "'I will sell them,' Boko Haram leader says of kidnapped Nigerian girls,"

If one is taught to believe they are to follow any particular holy scripture, is it surprising at all to find individuals following not just the good parts, but all parts? Muhammad was an avid collector of human beings, often selling them as well. As a Muslim, you're often taught to live in the way of Muhammad. If Muhammad believed he was doing right by Allah, Shekau may also believe the same thing, as well as others who follow Boko Haram.

This ought to send a message to moderate religious individuals, who hold up the very books and ideas used to justify the murder, abduction, rape, and slavery of human beings today; when the moderates do so, they are legitimizing the material the extremists use as a means to morally excuse their actions. This tragedy, at the present moment, is mostly unsolved. The girl's location is presently unknown, but efforts are still in progress.

Summary

This is not a fight between good and evil. This is a fight between ideas. These extremists hold ideas found within their Islamic doctrine; ideas many thought were long forgotten. The longer these texts are revered, the longer we'll bear witness to violence and ignorance. I truly believe these ideas can be easily forgotten; men who belong to groups like ISIL and Boko Haram may have been pleasant individuals if not for the ideology they follow. We can pull our species from the clutches of faith, but only if faith is for-

http://www.cnn.com/2014/05/05/world/africa/nigeria-abducted-girls/ (May 6, 2014) gotten. Sam Harris was correct when he stated Islam was the mother lode of bad ideas.[102] If we can inspire those of the future to cast aside nonsense, everything that I previously wrote in this chapter can be of the past and the past only.

---

[102] Adam Ericksen, Islam and the Mother Lode of Bad Ideas: The Bill Maher, Sam Harris, and Ben Affleck Debate,"
http://www.patheos.com/blogs/teachingnonviolentatonement/2014/10/isla
m-and-the-motherload-of-bad-ideas-the-bill-maher-sam-harris-and-ben-
affleck-debate/ (October 8, 2014)

CHAPTER FOUR
IN THE NAME OF CHRIST

It's often said that Christianity is a loving religion. Much like Islam, we find Christians the world over proclaiming Jesus taught only love and tolerance. We're also asked to believe that Christianity is a force for good and Christians, as a whole, are nice and well behaved people. They give to charities, volunteer in helping the hurt and needy, and give hope to those who may otherwise never find it. Christians believe they are a collection of truth-seekers; enemies of those who seek to derail society. *We have always been persecuted,* they may say. To the contrary, I would answer.

Christianity wasn't always as loving as most pretend it to be. There was a period in time in history where Christian tyranny reigned supreme. Blood was shed, lives were lost, and humanity was all together minimalized as a result of the institutionalization of dogmatic, archaic, and brutal teachings. Ignorance dominated the landscape; stupidity and superstition were paraded as things of virtue, when in fact they are quite not. Christianity rose to be one of the most followed religions not by the truth of its claims but by the sharpness of the end of its bloody sword. Christianity has never proved to be a means to make the world a better place. I would contend, however, that if not for the inception of Christian teachings, the world would be a much better place.

The First Crusade

The Crusades was a rather violent collection of wars between the eleventh and thirteenth centuries. During that time, Muslims controlled the Holy Land and Jerusalem and Pope Urban II wanted to desperately reclaim the territory. With religious ideologies driving the wars between the Christians and Muslims, it's hard to find any other appropriate motivating factor. What made these wars particularly interesting was the way in which the Christians savagely assaulted their enemies; reminiscent of the way God commanded Joshua in the Old Testament.

During the first crusade, Raymond of Agiles wrote vividly about what transpired during the siege of 1099. He wrote:

"Some of our men cut off the heads of their enemies. Others shot them with arrows, so that they fell from the towers. Others tortured them longer by casting them into the flames. Piles of heads, hands, and feet were to be seen in the streets of the city. One had to pick one's way over the bodies of men and horses. But these were small matters compared to what happened at the Temple of Solomon. You would not believe it if I told you. Suffice to say that in the Temple and porch of Solomon men rode in blood up to their knees and bridle reins. Indeed, it was a just and splendid judgment of God that this place should be filled with the blood of the unbelievers, since it had suffered so long from their blasphemies."[103]

---

[103] Morris Bishop, *The Middle Ages*. Boston: Houghton Mifflin, 2001. Print.

Fulcher of Chartres, a priest from the first crusade, also wrote:

"Some Saracens, Arabs, and Ethiopians took refuge in the tower of David, others fled to the temples of the Lord and of Solomon. A great fight took place in the court and porch of the temples, where they were unable to escape from our gladiators. Many fled to the roof of the temple of Solomon, and were shot with arrows, so that they fell to the ground dead. In this temple almost ten thousand were killed. Indeed, if you had been there you would have seen our feet colored to our ankles with the blood of the slain. But what more shall I relate? None of them were left alive; neither women nor children were spared."[104]

Faith knows no bounds, allowing those who believe with the utmost conviction the permission to commit disgusting acts of violence. War is a terrible thing, in any situation, but there is such a thing as "over-kill" and that was what happened during the first crusade; a particularly nasty fight of barbaric proportions. What else should one expect from a collection of violent, superstitious men who wish to entertain their religious fantasies?

I say, we should expect nothing more and nothing less. The remaining years of fighting went along the same lines; bloodshed and intolerance. Had the Christians not attacked, innocent lives would have been spared. Eventually, the Christian forces retreated, leaving the Muslim population in victory but in ruins at the same time.

---

[104] "Fulcher of Chartres: History of the Expedition to Jerusalem," Fordham University, http://legacy.fordham.edu/halsall/source/fulcher-cde.asp#capture

The Spanish Inquisition

Toward the end of the 15th century, Spain was home to torture and death, all in the name of Christ. During that time, the Catholic Church organized a series of trials that was meant to expel those of different faiths from the region; whether through exile, cruel systems of punishment, and death, the church persistently culled the non-Catholics from the herd, particularly Protestants and Jews. Pope Sixtus had ordered Spain to follow a particular code of conduct regarding the inquisition if the trials were to be executed, but King Ferdinand intervened. He felt the trials were too confined, which ultimately led to the torture and deaths of many innocent men and women.

Those who found themselves awaiting trial were often met with sadistic forms of punishment, such as waterboarding, hanging from chains, stretched on what is commonly called "the rack," beaten, and starved. Due to the adverse conditions many were subjected to, most were met with death before they reached trial.

If one actually made it to trial, there were a number of available outcomes. If they were found guilty, sometimes they were forced to pay an exuberant amount of money to the church and they would have been publically humiliated as a result of their non-Catholicism. Sometimes they were sentenced to more torturous punishment and may or may not have their property seized by the Catholic Church. Some were also executed by the Spanish government, particularly burning at the stake in most cases.

The Spanish Inquisition formally ended in 1836. While only close to 1,300 people were believed to have been executed compared to the almost 80,000 charges formally filed, there is no greater saddening realization than that of how those innocent individuals must have felt. To be afraid, beaten, and alone is a frightening thought; instances that which could have been avoided had those who perpetrated such idiocy had cast aside their silly and dogmatic ideologies. I do not hate those of faith; I wouldn't even wish death upon those who do believe. I care far too much for humanity to allow myself such beliefs. However, if a society collectively and dogmatically follows an ancient book, these sorts of things tend to happen.

Pope John Paul II eventually issued an apology, recognizing the failings of the Catholic Church during that dark period of history. In 1994, he stated:

"Hence it is appropriate that as the second millennium of Christianity draws to a close the Church should become ever more fully conscious of the sinfulness of her children, recalling all those times in history when they departed from the spirit of Christ and His Gospel and, instead of offering to the world the witness of a life inspired by the values of her faith, indulged in ways of thinking and acting which were truly forms of counter-witness and scandal. Although she is holy because of her incorporation into Christ, the Church does not tire of doing penance. Before God and man, she always acknowledges as her own her sinful sons and daughters."[105]

---

[105] Pope John Paul II, "TERTIO MILLENNIO ADVENIENTE," http://www.cin.org/jp2ency/tertmill.html (November 1994)

The apology is weak, at best. There is nothing that can formally excuse the actions of those from the church's past. We as secularists must never forget the horrors committed during the Spanish Inquisition, as well as all other inquisitions established throughout the world during that time. Inquisitions were also established in countries such as Rome and Italy, adding to the already horrifying acts of violence and rage. Remember these moments the next time someone tells you faith is harmless.

The Spanish Requirement of 1513

Christian theology played a key role in the conquest of the Americas. The Spanish Requirement of 1513 was passed by the Spanish Monarchy, which gave the Spanish the right to stake a claim on all land and seize such from any inhabiting humans. Christian beliefs maintain the idea that the world belongs to that of the "chosen people" and all such humans that do not fall into that category, essentially non-Catholics, have no right to anything, let alone property and even autonomy. The document that gave such an arrogant "divine right" goes as such:

"On the part of the King, Don Fernando, and of Doña Juana, his daughter, Queen of Castile and León, subduers of the barbarous nations, we their servants notify and make known to you, as best we can, that the Lord our God, living and eternal, created the heaven and the earth, and one man and one woman, of whom you and we, and all the men of the world, were and are all descendants, and all those who come after us.

Of all these nations God our Lord gave charge to one man, called St. Peter, that he should be lord and superior of all the men in the world, that all should obey him, and that he should be the head of the whole human race, wherever men should live, and under whatever law, sect, or belief they should be; and he gave him the world for his kingdom and jurisdiction.

One of these pontiffs, who succeeded St. Peter as lord of the world in the dignity and seat which I have before mentioned, made donation of these isles and Terra-firma to the aforesaid King and Queen and to their successors, our lords, with all that there are in these territories,

Wherefore, as best we can, we ask and require you that you consider what we have said to you, and that you take the time that shall be necessary to understand and deliberate upon it, and that you acknowledge the Church as the ruler and superior of the whole world,

But if you do not do this, and maliciously make delay in it, I certify to you that, with the help of God, we shall powerfully enter into your country, and shall make war against you in all ways and manners that we can, and shall subject you to the yoke and obedience of the Church and of their highnesses; we shall take you, and your wives, and your children, and shall make slaves of them, and as such shall sell and dispose of them as their highnesses may command; and we shall take away your goods, and shall do you all the mischief and damage that we can, as to vassals who do not obey, and refuse to receive their lord, and resist and contradict him: and we protest that the deaths and losses which shall accrue from this are your fault, and not that of their highnesses, or ours, nor of these cavaliers who come with us ."[106]

This document was to be relayed to those whom the Spanish encountered, and the results were often terrifying. One particularly vile conquest was that of the overthrow of the Aztec Empire in 1519. Hernando Cortes intended to convert the native people to Catholicism but was met with resistance as he found communication to be completely unobtainable. They also found the Aztecs sacrifice of human beings to be appalling and reprehensible.

Bernal Diaz del Castillo, who fought alongside Cortes, described his experience of witnessing how the Aztecs disposed of those who they sacrificed. In *True History of the Conquest of New Spain,* he wrote:

"At the very top of the cue [temple] there was another alcove, the woodwork of which was very finely carved, and here there was another image, half man and half lizard, encrusted with precious stones, with half its body covered in a cloak. Here too all was covered with blood, both walls and altar, and the stench was such that we could hardly wait to get out. They kept a large drum there, and when they beat it the sound was most dismal, like some music from the infernal regions, as you might say, and it could be heard six miles away. In that small platform were many more diabolical objects, trumpets great and small, and large knives, and many hearts that had been burnt with incense before their idols; and everything was caked with blood. The stench here too was like a

---

[106] "AD 1513: El Requierimento: Spain demands subservience," Native Voices http://www.nlm.nih.gov/nativevoices/timeline/178.html

slaughter-house, and we could scarcely stay in the place."[107]

After a series of battles, Cortes finally conquered the Aztec Empire. I will agree that human sacrifice is barbaric and unnecessary, but they too were acting on religious beliefs. Castillo failed to see the hypocrisy in his own position; as they attempted to force-convert an entire civilization, he found no fault in that. Why? Perhaps it was because he believed he belonged to the one true religion. Spain, Cortes, and the forced conversions and territory claiming resulted from religious ideology just the same as human sacrifice resulted from religious ideologies; one, in my opinion, is as wicked as the other.

Slavery

The Bible speaks openly in regards to keeping slaves; it may not surprise those who've studied the region from which these texts derive. When they were written, slavery was common place. That, of course, is not to say that it was okay even in ancient times. We were infantile in social groups. Humans were still learning then; hell, we're still learning. We understand now that owning other human beings is wrong, and I'll suggest we would have discovered this sooner if not for those who believed they were correct in the eyes of their god. What does the Old Testament say about slavery? The book states:

---

[107] Bernal Diaz del Castillo, *The True History of The Conquest of New Spain*

"If thou buy an Hebrew servant, six years he shall serve: and in the seventh he shall go out free for nothing. If he came in by himself, he shall go out by himself: if he were married, then his wife shall go out with him. If his master have given him a wife, and she have born him sons or daughters; the wife and her children shall be her master's, and he shall go out by himself. And if the servant shall plainly say, I love my master, my wife, and my children; I will not go out free. Then his master shall bring him unto the judges; he shall also bring him to the door, or unto the door post; and his master shall bore his ear through with an aul; and he shall serve him for ever."[108]

"Both thy bondmen, and thy bondmaids, which thou shalt have, shall be of the heathen that are round about you; of them shall ye buy bondmen and bondmaids. Moreover of the children of the strangers that do sojourn among you, of them shall ye buy, and of their families that are with you, which they begat in your land: and they shall be your possession. And ye shall take them as an inheritance for your children after you, to inherit them for a possession; they shall be your bondmen forever: but over your brethren the children of Israel, ye shall not rule one over another with rigour."[109]

How does the Bible ask one to treat their slave? The book states:

"And if a man smite his servant, or his maid, with a rod, and he die under his hand; he shall be surely

---

[108] Exodus 21:2-6 KJV
[109] Leviticus 25:44-46 KJV

punished. Notwithstanding, if he continues a day or two, he shall not be punished: for he is his money."[110]

What about the New Testament? The book states:

"Servants, be obedient to them that are your masters according to the flesh, with fear and trembling, in singleness of your heart, as unto Christ."[111]

"Let as many servants as are under the yoke count their own masters worthy of all honour, that the name of God and his doctrine be not blasphemed. And they that have believing masters, let them not despise them, because they are brethren; but rather do them service, because they are faithful and beloved, partakers of the benefit. These things teach and exhort."[112]

These texts represent an ancient culture from which we should learn from, not idolize. They were guilty of crimes unspeakably evil by today's standards, which is now much more progressive than the ideologies of those from the past.

In the United States, slavery was permitted in its early years. If not for the Emancipation Proclamation and the tireless efforts of Abraham Lincoln and the abolitionists, it may've taken much longer for our society to reach a more humanistic and pleasant approach to the treating of other human beings. I do not wish to ignore those who had, in fact, opposed the owning of other human beings. Those very people had also used biblical text to stand for the abolishment of slavery, dating as far back as when the very first set-

---

[110] Exodus 21:20-21
[111] Ephesians 6:5
[112] 1 Timothy 6:1-2

tlers of North America landed on the shores of the East Coast; everyone gunning for their own beliefs without realizing the hypocrisy. In the Emancipation Proclamation, it states:

"And by virtue of the power, and for the purpose aforesaid, I do order and declare that all persons held as slaves within said designated States, and parts of States, are, and henceforward shall be free; and that the Executive government of the United States, including the military and naval authorities thereof, will recognize and maintain the freedom of said persons…And upon this act, sincerely believed to be an act of justice, warranted by the Constitution, upon military necessity, I invoke the considerate judgment of mankind, and the gracious favor of Almighty God."[113]

However, slave owners believed slavery would free the Africans from their wicked ways if also indoctrinated with Christianity, of course.

I spoke briefly about the conquests of the Americas. I had not mentioned Christopher Columbus, who sailed much of the Americas during the late 1400's. He is often revered by some as a hero, others consider him a pillager and slave-trader. He wrote extensively during his time at sea. In one such journal, he quoted his admiral as saying of the native people:

"It appears to me, that the people are ingenious, and would be good servants and I am of opinion that they would very readily become Christians, as they appear

---

[113] Abraham Lincoln, "The Emancipation Proclomation," http://www.archives.gov/exhibits/featured_documents/emancipation_proc lamation/transcript.html

to have no religion. They very quickly learn such words as are spoken to them. If it please our Lord, I intend at my return to carry home six of them to your Highnesses, that they may learn our language."[114]

Forced conversion and servitude, aside from ascertaining land forcefully, was an objective of those whom Columbus traveled with.

Christianity certainly does not prohibit the owning of slaves. We as human beings ought to recognize when we have failed as civilized creatures; the problem with this is, most do not even realize they are acting uncivilized. Slave owners of the past thought they were civilized, doing God's work, much the same as the jihadists today believe they are doing the work of Allah. Slavery, in most forms, may be gone as far as we have come to understand, but let us not forget the role Christianity played propagating that bad idea in the past.

Anti-Semitism

Throughout the course of Christianity, anti-Semitism has run rampant throughout, from the highest point to its very lowest. To be anti-Semitic is, to put it simply, to be prejudice against those who identify as Jewish. Now, anti-Semitism can be expressed in religious, cultural, and nationalistic terms, meaning the hatred of the Jewish people extends further than simply religious context. In this passage, I will mainly focus on the discrimination toward the Jewish people on part of the Christian church.

---

[114] Christopher Columbus,
http://legacy.fordham.edu/halsall/source/columbus1.asp

Christian anti-Semitism is rooted deeply in the religion's history, dating back to the writings of Paul. In 1 Thessalonians, Paul tells the reader how the Jewish people were handled after Christ's death and he even expresses his own disgust of them. In it, he states:

"For ye, brethren, became followers of the churches of God which in Judaea are in Christ Jesus: for ye also have suffered like things of your own countrymen, even as they have of the Jews: Who both killed the Lord Jesus, and their own prophets, and have persecuted us; and they please not God, and are contrary to all men: Forbidding us to speak to the Gentiles that they might be saved, to fill up their sins alway: for the wrath is come upon them to the uttermost."[115]

Later, the negative views of the Jews began with Constantine and the Council of Nicea. During his speech, he stated:

"Let us then have nothing in common with the detestable Jewish crowd; for we have received from our Savior a different way. A course at once legitimate and honorable lies open to our most holy religion. Beloved brethren, let us with one consent adopt this course, and withdraw ourselves from all participation in their baseness. For their boast is absurd indeed, that it is not in our power without instruction from them to observe these things..."[116]

---

[115] 1 Thessalonians 2:14-16
[116] "Texts from the History of the Relationship," Council of Centers on Jewish-Christian Relations, http://www.ccjr.us/dialogika-resources/primary-texts-from-the-history-of-the-relationship/246-constantine-i

Almost 100 years later, the Roman Empire formally recognized Christianity as the state-recognized religion in 438; essentially, making it illegal to practice any other religion. In the Theodosian Code, put in to law under the reign of Theodosius II. Basically, it is really a combination of two separate codes written prior to the existence of the Theodosian Code. It wasn't until 592 when a document called the Justinian Code was put into practice.

This document differed from the Theodosian code, in regards to the state religion, by actually defining those who did not practice Christianity as noncitizens. In the portion known as the Codex, it strips the Jewish people of many rights, including the right to practice Judaism, speaking in Hebrew, publicly testify against Christians, and inheriting property from family members who called themselves Christian. This set in stone the future of the Jewish people in Europe for centuries to come.

During the Medieval period of history, Jews faced many hardships. The Black Death, perhaps the worst event to hit humanity, killed millions of people all throughout Europe. As superstitious people do, the population, which was predominantly Christian, sought to find an answer. Since the science wasn't available, the people presumed the spread of the disease was attributed to God and his anger. Many "causes" were presented, one of which being the existing practice of Judaism. According to the Website of Fordham University, Jews were subjected to death as a result of the growing anti-Semitism and the rising body count due to the spread of the bubonic plague. On the website, it states:

"By authority of Amadeus VI, Count of Savoy, a number of the Jews who lived on the shores of Lake Geneva, having been arrested and put to the torture, naturally confessed anything their inquisitors suggested. These Jews, under torture, incriminated others. Records of their confessions were sent from one town to another in Switzerland and down the Rhine River into Germany, and as a result, thousands of Jews, in at least two hundred towns and hamlets, were butchered and burnt."[117]

Sadly, these poor individuals lost their lives as a result of Christian religious beliefs. If only their god had given them in scripture the germ theory of disease, this may have been prevented. Yes, the previous statement was a bit tongue-in-cheek, but it still stands as a testament to the non-legitimacy of religion and the beliefs there of. Superstition grows where ignorance lives. If allowed to breed without check, lives will be certainly lost, just as history has proved.

Later in history, the Catholic Church made many attempts to separate itself from the anti-Semitism spreading throughout the continent. However, that wouldn't stop many popes reinstating the idea that Jewish people were less than human. This, I would argue, allowed that terrible idea to prosper, giving rise to Adolf Hitler's beliefs regarding anti-Semitism and his need to purge society of Judaism. Hitler truly believed he was doing the will of his god by taking the fight to the Jewish people. In Mein Kampf, he wrote:

---

[117] "Jewish History Sourcebook: The Black Death and the Jews 1348-1349 CE," Fordham University, http://legacy.fordham.edu/halsall/jewish/1348-jewsblackdeath.asp

"Hence today I believe that I am acting in accordance with the will of the Almighty Creator: by defending myself against the Jew, I am fighting for the work of the Lord."[118]

In his autobiography, he made many, many more comments expressing his hatred of Jews and their practices. Hitler later gained political power in Germany, allowing him to follow through with his plan to eradicate the Jewish people, resulting in the holocaust.

After his reign of terror ended, roughly 6 million Jewish people were killed. It is true that many Christian's beliefs during that time did not align with that of Hitler's, but could he have accomplished such a disgusting feat if the population had refused to follow his orders? I would like to believe the answer would have been no, but subservience is common among Christianity and the willingness to think for oneself is completely discouraged. Religious beliefs, particularly Christian beliefs, allow the believer to suspend personal accountability. Thus, resulting in the inability to stand against all that is wrong. What Hitler and his regime accomplished was atrocious, as was his given allowance to continue the genocide of the Jewish people.

Christian Terrorism

Christian beliefs do not correspond with reality, meaning they have yet to meet the burden of proof that would allow those beliefs to hold merit. Individuals are free to entertain those beliefs, as I expressed in

---

[118] "Adolf Hitler: Excerpts from Mein Kampf," Jewish Virtual Library, https://www.jewishvirtuallibrary.org/jsource/Holocaust/kampf.html

my opening chapter. I find those in error who wish to impose such beliefs on the general population; the global population, in its entirety, does not self-identify as Christian. That being said, we mustn't allow those who believe those things to bully the rest into submission. As for the United States, this nation is a secular nation; our government does not directly identify with any particular religion. Thus, our government cannot uphold a standard or standards based on theological principles. When this is met, there is push back from Christian fundamentalists. Sometimes, that push-back can be rather violent.

The Ku Klux Klan was formally established in the United States in the late 1860's as a white supremacy movement. Three distinct movements have defined the KKK's existence throughout history, from the 1865 to 1871, the second movement from 1915 to 1944, and from 1946 to the present day. This organization justifies their racism by citing religious beliefs. Michael Fisher of Washington and Lee University says:

"The Ku Klux Klan is composed entirely of white, Anglo-Saxon, Christian American citizens, both male and female, who believe that their race and religion are superior to those of people of other colors and religions...The Klan takes direct action against those who do not share its beliefs or those who it simply views as inferior based on its readings of the Bible. Klansmen recognize the differences of other groups and translate them into justification for hate."[119]

---

[119] Michael Fisher, "The Ku Klux Klan,"
http://home.wlu.edu/~lubint/touchstone/KKK-Fisher.htm

J. Keith Akins of New Mexico State University also says:

"Traditionally, the Ku Klux Klan has held extremely conservative Protestant Christian beliefs. Since the early 1970s, many Klaverns have converted to strongly fundamentalist Protestant beliefs, Christian Identity beliefs, or an amalgam of the two."[120]

He then goes on to explain Christian Identity as so:

"Christian Identity, which has become popular among many Klan groups, is a relatively obscure sect known primarily for its racism and anti-Semitism. Its core belief is that whites are actually descendants of the Biblical lost tribes of Israel and are therefore God's "Chosen People." Most Identity adherents believe that Jews, in contrast, are descended from Satan and that other nonwhite peoples are "mud" people on the same spiritual level as animals."[121]

The KKK was formally recognized as a terrorist group in 1870 because a number of Klansmen were found guilty of acts which were incredibly violent in nature. As a result, the organization slowly began to dwindle. It was then recreated in the early 1900s, which was when the organization reached its highest numbers, reaching over 3,000,000 in membership; the time in which their crimes against humanity soared.

---

[120] J. Keith Akins, "The Ku Klux Klan: America's Forgotten Terrorists," http://www.uhv.edu/asa/articles/KKKAmericasForgottenTerrorists.pdf (2006)

[121] J. Keith Akins, "The Ku Klux Klan: America's Forgotten Terrorists," http://www.uhv.edu/asa/articles/KKKAmericasForgottenTerrorists.pdf (2006)

During the 1950s and 1960s, the KKK engaged in a number of terrorist related acts. In 1951, the home of NAACP activists Harold and Harriette Moore in Florida was bombed, resulting in their deaths. Medgar Evers, another civil rights activist, was shot to death outside of his home in 1963; this incident was cinematically portrayed in the film *Ghosts of Mississippi*. In that same year, the 16th Street Baptist Church was bombed by four Klansmen, killing four young African American girls. The KKK not only targeted African Americans, they targeted anyone who stood for the rights of African Americans. In 1966, three civil rights activists, two of which were Caucasian, were kidnapped and murdered by Klansmen. This, of course, does not outshine the vast number of people individually lynched by Klansmen all throughout the United States.

Those above are just a few of the most well-known cases, which only slightly demonstrate how in which terrible religious beliefs can foster hatred and violence. This being the very reason why I oppose religion the most perhaps; Christians often maintain there is a spiritual divide: those who are God's people and those who aren't. For the men and women of the Ku Klux Klan, African Americans are less than human based on beliefs formed from pronouncements made throughout the Bible. If not for those beliefs, a countless number of lives may have been spared.

The same can be said for those who have violently opposed the right for a woman to have an abortion. They do so based on biblical principles, defining the very act of aborting a fetus as murder. Believing the fetus is given a soul by God, though the religious can never give a concise answer as to when a soul enters the embryo as Sam Harris has point out, the practice of abortion has been protested against by those from the Christian community. For instance, the Catholic Answers website[122] cites these passages from the Bible:

"Thine hands have made me and fashioned me together round about; yet thou dost destroy me."[123]

"But thou art he that took me out of the womb: thou didst make me hope when I was upon my mother's breasts. I was cast upon thee from the womb: thou art my God from my mother's belly."[124]

"For thou hast possessed my reins: thou hast covered me in my mother's womb. I will praise thee; for I am fearfully and wonderfully made: marvelous are thy works; and that my soul knoweth right well. My substance was not hid from thee, when I was made in secret, and curiously wrought in the lowest parts of the earth."[125]

"Thus saith the Lord that made thee, and formed thee from the womb, which will help thee; Fear not, O Jacob, my servant; and thou, Jesurun, whom I have chosen."[126]

"And it came to pass, that, when Elisabeth heard the salutation of Mary, the babe leaped in her womb; and Elisabeth was filled with the Holy Ghost."[127]

---

[122] Peggy Frye, "Where in the Bible does it say that abortion is wrong?" Catholic Answers, http://www.catholic.com/quickquestions/where-in-the-Bible-does-it-say-that-abortion-is-wrong
[123] Job 10:8 KJV
[124] Psalms 22:9-10
[125] Psalms 139:13-15
[126] Isaiah 44:2
[127] Luke 1:41

"And not only this; but when Rebecca also had conceived by one, even by our father Isaac; (For the children being not yet born, neither having done any good or evil, that the purpose of God according to election might stand, not of works, but of him that calleth;)"[128]

Contextually, these do not address abortion specifically. Those who hold ideas outside of their theology, they sometimes seek answers within their religion's doctrine because they believe those writings could somehow offer solutions to modern predicaments. As far as the soul is concerned, we are unable to determine whether a soul gives human beings life; as far as we can observe, a working brain is needed to experience life. CARM, the website of Christian apologist Matt Slick, states:

"The Bible definitely teaches that the unborn are persons because the unborn possess personal attributes, are described by personal pronouns, Jesus is called a child at conception, the unborn are called children, are protected by the same punishment as for adults, are called by God before birth, and are known personally by God just like any other person."[129]

What we have discovered is, using top-down logic, the brain creates consciousness, and consciousness then allows us to perceive reality. All that we understand about the human experience depends on consciousness which is derived from a functioning nerv-

---

[128] Romans 9:10-11
[129] Ryan Turner, "What does the Bible say about abortion?" CARM, https://carm.org/Bible-abortion

ous system. For that reason, we have no grounds to consider abortion murder, as I talked about earlier in this book. Life is defined differently by both the scientific community and the theological community; one of these is the only one who has yet to present any evidence, and the other relies of faith. I'm sorry, but ones religious beliefs hold no merit as far as the discussion has gone so far.

Because of this, Christian fundamentalists have taken action into their own hands, "protecting" the innocent unborn children from who they believe to be murderers. I believe these individuals arrive on this conclusion in a purely emotional way. We are social species, so it's to no surprise that many believe that a fetus is, in fact, a human being with rights. They go further by believing those lives are a creation of God. They are, in a sense, doing their god's will by attacking those who provide abortions.

A number of abortion doctors and staff members have been murdered because of these individuals. In 1993, Dr. David Gunn was fatally shot to death by Michael Griffin, a former member of the Ku Klux Klan. In 1994, Dr. John Britton and James Barret were murdered by the Reverend Paul Jennings Hill, who died by lethal injection still believing he was doing his god's work. His last words were:

"The last thing I want to say: If you believe abortion is a lethal force, you should oppose the force and do what you have to do to stop it. May God help you to protect the unborn as you would want to be protected."[130]

---

[130] "Paul Jennings Hill," Clark County Prosecutor, http://www.clarkprosecutor.org/html/death/US/hill873.htm

In 1998, Dr. Barnett Slepian was shot to death in his home by James Kopp, who considered himself a militant Roman Catholic. The most well-known murder is that of George Tiller. He was one of the few practicing doctors who provided late term abortions in the United States. Because of this, he was well-known among those who were a part of the anti-abortion movement. As he was leaving his church on a Sunday morning in 2009, he was shot to death by Scott Roeder, who was somewhat involved in the group Operation Rescue; an organization established to fight against abortion providers. These are just a portion of those murdered by Christian anti-abortion activists.

Christian fundamentalists not only engaged in murder, they also engaged in arson, physical assaults, and bombing attacks. In 2011, the National Abortion Federations released statistics regarding instances of violence against abortion doctors and clinics. According to the document, which gives statistics from 1977 to 2009 in the United States and Canada, 41 buildings were bombed, 175 instances of arson, 100 individuals were assaulted with acid, 1,400 acts of vandalism, and 1,993 acts of trespassing. These numbers do not begin to touch the amount of threats received, which totals 16,189; this number includes death threats, threats of anthrax attacks, harassing telephone calls and emails, faux bomb devices, and bomb threats.[131]

[131] NAF Violence and Disruption Statistics: Incidents of Violence & Disruption Against Abortion Providers in the U.S. & Canada," http://prochoice.org/wp-content/uploads/violence_stats.pdf

Summary

There are those that say, of all faiths, when people engage in wrongdoing, and specifically cite their faith as a motivating factor, they are not representing the religion as a whole. That is fine to claim that, but with that we cannot also accept the good done by those of faith then either; the religious want their cake and eat it too. It's either all or nothing. Throughout the history of Christianity and Christian teaching, thousands upon thousands have either been harmed or killed as a result of those who claim divine warrant in doing so.

As I wrote earlier, yes, religious people do good deeds because of their faith, but Christianity is often described as a loving peaceful religion. I believe, what they mean to say is this: Most of us are loving and peaceful. I contend those individuals would be loving and peaceful even without their religious faith. Those who commit violence in the name of Christ, on the other hand, may not have done so if not for the doctrine they hold so dearly.

CHAPTER FIVE
JUNK SCIENCE

Science is a wonderful thing. It provides us with answers we may have otherwise been unable to obtain. Its practitioners use reason and logic to formulate their hypotheses, carefully perform experiments and collect important data, and thus alleviating the mysteries of life's many questions. I believe religion predates modern science as a means to understand the natural world. Faith, a belief without evidence, separates itself from the scientific community in a large way; one should not believe something without sufficient evidence, meaning it is okay to say "I don't know." That sometimes does not sit well with those who have faith in a deity.

We understand the big bang, but we don't know for certain what existed prior to that. The religious say, "My god created it." We understand evolution, but we don't know for certain how life began. The religious say, "My god created it." The same can be said for medicine, or the practice of modern medicine, rather. The religious believe their god has the power to perform miracle and heal the lame. Yet, the opposite has proven to be true. This is why science and medicine often butt heads with religion so often.

Sometimes, the religious claim science and medicine have gotten things wrong. That is fine; as I've said before, one is free to believe anything they so choose to. It is a completely different game once one wishes to impose those things on the general populace. In this chapter I will discuss these battles; the struggles between reality and superstition and nonsense. It's often said these individuals have been indoctrinated, that they really have no way to tell the difference between their faith and reality and it's not their fault. There is, in fact, a difference between being ignorant and being willfully ignorant. If the information is available, one has no good reason to align their views of reality with those of the ancient world. While this chapter may lack in length, I will surely address the long history of conflict between religion and the practices of science and medicine.

Evolution, Creationism, and Public Education

Creationism is the idea that god, or any divine being, created the universe and life. So far as we're able to tell, this is idea holds no merit. Any attempt at legitimizing this claim has failed miserably. I'll steer away from refuting creationism all together as I have already covered that issue in my book *Improbable: Issues with the God Hypothesis*. I, at one time, entertained the idea that the biblical account of creation could possibly be true. Unfortunately, as I began to research the subject, I found no credible evidence to support the idea that anything had been divinely conjured. As it turns out, no one else, including the religious, has either. This is the very reason why we'll never find creationism being taught to public school children; which is a great thing, I must add. In the United States, the public school system is supported by the taxes of the general community. Since creationism is a religious notion, and because we are a secular nation, school systems are not allowed to teach religious beliefs as fact.

One of the three most important cases in regards to this topic in the United States is the Scopes trial of 1925. It began in Tennessee when the Butler Act was put into law, which made it so that public school systems were required to teach the biblical creation account as science to students. This, again, is a display of the undereducated attempting to pass legislation supporting the beliefs they hold. Butler was once quoted as saying:

"I read in the papers that boys and girls were coming home from school and telling their fathers and mothers that the Bible was all nonsense. When the bill passed, I naturally thought we wouldn't hear any more about evolution in Tennessee."[132]

That was until John Scopes entered the scene. He was a substitute teacher who had apparently violated the Butler Act, bringing about this famous court case. Scopes was eventually found guilty because the judge had to comply with the Butler Act, but the conviction was overturned due to a technicality, thus allowing Scope's lawyers to appeal the case in the Tennessee Supreme Court. While Scopes and his lawyers lost the appealed case, it sparked a debate that would eventually call into questions a number of other anti-evolution bills throughout the United States.

In 1968, the United States Supreme Court entertained the case Epperson vs. Arkansas. Susan Ep-

---

[132] Abraham Hill Gibson, "Confronting the Tree of Life: Three Court Cases in Modern American History," http://scholar.lib.vt.edu/theses/available/etd-05122008-131342/unrestricted/AbeGibsonThesis.pdf (April 28, 2008)

person was afraid she'd be found guilty of violating Arkansas' anti-evolution law because she believed the text books she was provided would put her in danger. She filed in Arkansas' Chancery Court, which agreed the law violated the First Amendment. Different from how the Scopes trial went, the Arkansas Supreme Court disagreed with the initial judge's findings. Also different from the Scopes trial, Epperson and her lawyers appealed to the United States Supreme Court, taking the fight to Washington D.C. With a much better result, the United States Supreme Court ruled that bills similar to the Butler act, of which Arkansas had on the books, were unconstitutional because they violated the First Amendment which states:

"Congress shall make no law respecting an establishment of religion, or prohibiting the free exercise thereof; or abridging the freedom of speech, or of the press; or the right of the people peaceably to assemble, and to petition the government for a redress of grievances."[133]

That being ruled, it gave others the right to fight against other anti-evolution bills in effect throughout the United States.

In the case titled Edwards vs. Aguillard, which took place in 1987, the United States Supreme Court was to rule on whether evolution should be taught alongside creationism, in which both sides of the conversation can be heard. As I said earlier, there is no other side. Creationism holds no merit, but what was most important is this: Creationism belongs to a specific religious ideology. This case was brought about

---

[133] "First Amendment," Cornell University Law School, https://www.law.cornell.edu/constitution/first_amendment

because Louisiana did have a law required the afore-mentioned situation, forcing all students to study biblical creation as well as evolution. As part of the ruling, the United States Supreme Court stated:

"Indeed, the Court acknowledged in Stone that its decision forbidding the posting of the Ten Commandments did not mean that no use could ever be made of the Ten Commandments, or that the Ten Commandments played an exclusively religious role in the history of Western Civilization. (449 U.S. at 42) In a similar way, teaching a variety of scientific theories about the origins of humankind to schoolchildren might be validly done with the clear secular intent of enhancing the effectiveness of science instruction."[134]

Sadly for those who wished to push their religious beliefs on those who had no other choice, the Court ruled against them.

With these rulings standing, it's been virtually impossible for the teaching of Christian based anti-evolution material in public schools. So how have the religious tried to interject the idea of biblical creation once again? The only way to do so was to try to strip Creationism of its biblical confines. This is what they consider intelligent design. The Discovery Institute defines intelligent design as:

"The theory of intelligent design holds that certain features of the universe and of living things are best

---

[134] "Edwards v. Aguillard," Cornell University Law School, https://www.law.cornell.edu/supremecourt/text/482/578

explained by an intelligent cause, not an undirected process such as natural selection."[135]

And how do they try to support the claim of a non-religious motive? The website claims intelligent design is, in fact, not creationism. It states:

"The theory of intelligent design is simply an effort to empirically detect whether the 'apparent design' in nature acknowledged by virtually all biologists is genuine design (the product of an intelligent cause) or is simply the product of an undirected process such as natural selection acting on random variations. Creationism typically starts with a religious text and tries to see how the findings of science can be reconciled to it. Intelligent design starts with the empirical evidence of nature and seeks to ascertain what inferences can be drawn from that evidence. Unlike creationism, the scientific theory of intelligent design does not claim that modern biology can identify whether the intelligent cause detected through science is supernatural"[136]

That would leave one to ask, "Who, or what, is this intelligent designer?" Well, as one may have expected, this topic was debated during the Kitzmiller vs. Dover Area School District case in 2005.

This case was brought as a result of a text book added to the curriculum of the public school, which taught intelligent design as an alternative science to the standard teaching of biology and evolution. Eventually, eleven parents challenged the public school

---

[135] "What is Intelligent Design?" Discovery Institute, http://www.intelligentdesign.org/whatisid.php
[136] "What is Intelligent Design?" Discovery Institute, http://www.intelligentdesign.org/whatisid.php

system, bringing the case to court. The plaintiffs brought a number of credible scientists as witnesses to help argue the case against intelligent design. The defendants, the county school board, brought Michael Behe as their main witness. After the proceedings ended, the court ruled in favor of the eleven parents, stating:

"The concept of intelligent design (hereinafter "ID"), in its current form, came into existence after the Edwards case was decided in 1987. For the reasons that follow, we conclude that the religious nature of ID would be readily apparent to an objective observer, adult or child...A significant aspect of the IDM [intelligent design movement] is that despite Defendants' protestations to the contrary, it describes ID as a religious argument. In that vein, the writings of leading ID proponents reveal that the designer postulated by their argument is the God of Christianity...ID's backers have sought to avoid the scientific scrutiny which we have now determined that it cannot withstand by advocating that the controversy, but not ID itself, should be taught in science class. This tactic is at best disingenuous, and at worst a canard. The goal of the IDM is not to encourage critical thought, but to foment a revolution which would supplant evolutionary theory with ID."[137]

Since this decision, other school board members have tried, and failed, to incorporate intelligent design with various public school systems.

---

[137] "Kitzmiller v. Dover Area School District," http://www.ucs.louisiana.edu/~ras2777/relpol/kitzmiller.htm (December 20, 2005)

The amount of dishonesty is both disgusting and not all that surprising. Where ever the religious are given the opportunity to push their views, particularly which of Christianity, we should assume they will. This is why most biblical teachings of science regarding the creation of life and the universe is often left in the hands of the home-schooling parent, giving them complete control over their child's, or children's, education. Thankfully enough, in recent years, a shift has occurred. Homeschooling parents are now more comfortable with teaching evolution, though it's not exclusive; evolution is being taught alongside creationism. "Guided" evolution is often what's represented.

One cannot argue against the claim that an unseen force guided evolution after the origin of life occurred, and since it is irrefutable, it's an intellectually dishonest position. It deserves no respect from anyone who wishes to consider them a rational person. Evolution is the best explanation for the diversity of life on this planet, which does not require a creator god to explain the function there of. Science, once again, trumps religious ideas revolving around the creation of the universe and life on Earth. Most of the world's countries have put a ban on the teaching of creationism, in any religious form, to children in the public school systems; it is even banned in countries like Iran, Brazil, and Pakistan. If these countries have no problem with the teaching of evolution, the state governments in the US should have no problem either.

Faith Healing and Prayer

Most have seen video footage of charismatic Christian preachers wailing and yelling, speaking in tongues, and even simply praying for their congregation. They are attempting to call upon the god it is they worship, believing he will bring to them good will. Most often, this is done when someone is either sick or they know of an individual who is quite sick. They believe their god can work wonders, healing them and their loved ones because they were righteous and holy servants of the lord. Even Jewish, Hindu, Shinto, and Muslim believers are all guilty of this. Where ever exists the belief in a deity or deities with healing powers, there will always be those who learn the hard way.

Of course, if someone prays or meditates and the person who was sick does get better, the believer will claim the power of their lord; all the while forgetting the inclusion, most often, of medical treatments. Those who do not seek medical help and instead depend primarily on faith and prayer, most often find their prayers and cries for help to be in vain. This terrible idea was well understood in the past, when no other source for treatment was available; even quirky herbal remedies were believed to heal a number of ailments. Today, that is a much different story. We have plenty of answers regarding the origins of many of today's common ailments and leading scientists and medical personnel in their particular fields have developed vaccines, treatments, and fitness plans meant to help the sick and keep the healthy in good shape.

Sometimes those who are affected by the ramifications of faith healing are those who had no other choice. Children are often forced to forego medical attention because their parents honestly believed their deity would "come to the rescue" and save them from the harm of a "fallen" world. Cases such as these come about so frequently it's often difficult to keep track. In America, the issue revolves around many state laws allowing parents to personally take their child's health in their own hands, particularly if it would interfere with their religious practices. In most cases, however, the parents are often charged with either murder or manslaughter; justice, of some sort, for those who have died.

I remember reading, not long ago, about a mother and a father who had sought prayer in the case involving their son and his bout with pneumonia. Herbert and Catherin Schaible refused to take their son to the doctor because they believed their god was taking care of the illness. Shockingly, this was not the first time a child of theirs died as a result of such neglectful behavior. In 2009, another son of theirs died also of pneumonia. According to the referring article, Herbert said:

"We believe in divine healing, that Jesus shed blood for our healing and that he died on the cross to break the devil's power."[138]

In both cases, simple antibiotics would've saved both of their children's lives. It's a shame that such a tragedy is so much more preventable, had faith and religious belief not been involved.

On February 5, 2013, Syble Rossiter died from complications due from type 1 diabetes. Her parents, Travis and Wenona, misunderstood her symptoms,

---

[138] Maggie Fox, "Doctor to Legislators: Refusing Medical Care Isn't Religious Freedom," http://www.nbcnews.com/health/kids-health/doctor-legislators-refusing-medical-care-isnt-religious-freedom-n320031 (March 9, 2015)

believing she was suffering from the flu. Instead of seeking a doctor, her parents resorted to prayer. They believed in the power of their god, that if they relied on him, everything would be alright. Travis even admitted that he felt doctors were for people with weak faith, and that if his daughter had asked for medical help, he would have talked her out of the decision.[139] Wenona had even experienced how faulty faith-based medical decisions were when her father believed prayer would save her seven year old brother from leukemia. In 1996, her brother died not long after the diagnosis. Sadly, Travis and Wenona finally learned just how weak prayer was. Their daughter was only twelve when she passed away.

In February of 2012, Austin Sprout died due to an infection from a burst appendix. Brandy and Russel Bellew also believed in the power of prayer, deriving such beliefs from their congregation, the General Assembly and the Church of the Firstborn. Luckily in Oregon, religious beliefs could no longer stand as a reasonable defense against a charge of manslaughter. As such, the parents pleaded guilty and received probation. This was not the first time tragedy struck the Sprout family. A number of years earlier, Austin's birth father died after seeking prayer rather than medical care. Evidently, Austin's mother still believed prayer and the power of her god could somehow save her son. He was sixteen when he passed away.

In August of 2003, Dwayne and Melta Schmidt believed their god would heal their newborn from a common post-birth infection. The child, Rhiana, was

---

[139] Kyle Odegard, "Opening arguments heard in faith healing couple's manslaughter trial," http://democratherald.com/news/local/crime-and-courts/opening-arguments-heard-in-faith-healing-couple-s-manslaughter-trial/article_87247f66-6492-11e4-8866-cfe056d4a497.html (November 4, 2014)

born in the family home. The couple was subsequently charged with reckless homicide for not seeking medical intervention. While testifying, Melta believed prayer had, in fact, been working. According to the referring article, the family attorney attempted to make a case for religious persecution. He said:

"My clients are being prosecuted as a result of their faith in God -- their religious beliefs...They didn't fail to act. They acted. They acted in accordance with their religious beliefs."[140]

While some may view their actions as admirable, I, as an antitheist and humanist, find it absolutely disgusting and irresponsible. If an adult chooses to make a decision that will alter their life course in the name of their faith, that is one thing. I don't enjoy seeing that either, but they are free to do as they please and if they wish to abstain from medicine, that is their prerogative. What frightens me the most, is when innocent children are subjected to the consequences of the irrational beliefs held by their parents. No child deserves to go through that. Rhiana was only two days old when she passed away.

Faith healing hasn't proven to work. In the cases in which it has been claimed to have worked, reality-based explanations are often available. Miracles may or may not happen, the truth of which is uncertain; so uncertain that relying on prayer can lead to catastrophically bad outcomes. Ones best bet is to always seek medical attention when needed, regardless of their faith. God may or may not exist, but medicine

---

140 "Parents Accused Of Letting Baby Die Untreated Found Guilty," Indy Channel, http://www.theindychannel.com/news/parents-accused-of-letting-baby-die-untreated-found-guilty (May 13, 2005.)

exists and has proven to help millions more than any god ever has.

Climate Change Denial

I fully acknowledge that a number of religious organizations fully support efforts to help alleviate the effects of climate change, but in this portion I wish to argue against an idea; one prevalent throughout all deity-based religious institutions. Those of faith sometimes believe Earth and all of its natural resources are ours to exploit. With reckless abandon, they'd wish to pillage and horde all the precious elements that help make their lives easier in this life. This idea is a pernicious one, free of science-based reasoning. To makes the matters worse, those who hold these silly ideas often have the power to pass legislation in favor of their faith.

In the United States, the Christian right, often composed of evangelical Christians, have made it quite clear they are not willing to change their opinion on the issues revolving around climate change. In 2012, one-time presidential candidate Rick Santorum said:

"If you leave it to Nature, then Nature will do what Nature does, which is boom and bust...We were put on this Earth as creatures of God to have dominion over the Earth, to use it wisely and steward it wisely, but for our benefit not for the Earth's benefit."[141]

Oklahoma Senator Jim Inhofe said in 2014:

---

[141] "Rick Santorum: I've Never Believed In The 'Hoax Of Global Warming'," *Huffington Post*, http://www.huffingtonpost.com/2012/02/07/rick-santorum-global-warming-hoax_n_1260168.html (February 7, 2012)

"God's still up there. The arrogance of people to think that we, human beings, would be able to change what He is doing in the climate is to me outrageous."[142]

Radio crazy-man Rush Limbaugh said in 2013:

"See, in my humble opinion, folks, if you believe in God, then intellectually you cannot believe in manmade global warming...You must be either agnostic or atheistic to believe that man controls something that he can't create."[143]

Bryan Fischer, radio host, dismissed climate change in 2014 by saying:

"People have been out there wringing their hands and trying to stir up all this agitation and fear because the oceans are going to rise, Manhattan is going to be under twenty feet of water, Hawaii is going to disappear under the waves...God says, 'Look, I am not going to destroy the earth with the waters of a flood ever again.'"[144]

In 2014, Tony Perkins of the Family Research Council said:

---

[142] Robert Lanham, "Inhofe's Greatest Climate Change Denial Hits," http://www.huffingtonpost.com/robert-lanham/james-inhofe-climate-change_b_6142170.html (November 12, 2014)
[143] Jack Jenkins, "Limbaugh: 'If You Believe In God, Then Intellectually You Cannot Believe In Manmade Global Warming'," http://thinkprogress.org/climate/2013/08/14/2469341/limbaugh-christians-global-warming/ (August 14, 2013)
[144] Kyle Mantyla, "Fischer: Rising Sea Levels Are Of No Concern Because God Will Never Destroy The Earth With Flood Waters," http://www.rightwingwatch.org/content/fischer-rising-sea-levels-are-no-concern-because-god-will-never-destroy-earth-flood-waters (September 19, 2014)

"I remember a few years ago, it might have been Jerry Falwell or Pat Robertson, made a reference to a hurricane or a storm being an act of God — it's interesting that's how we refer to some of these things in our insurance policies — they were ridiculed, saying 'how dumb can you be?' Well, there's more to back that up than to say what's happening in our environment, our climate, is because of people driving Suburbans or coal-fired power plants."[145]

If someone believes in an all-powerful god that has a plan, climate change will always seem silly. They must deny man-made climate change in order for their beliefs to conform to the evidence of reality. The climate is certainly changing, so for them, their god is simply changing it. So, to them, they believe it's meant to be. "Leave it to God," they'd say. This is why we should not respect bad ideas.

The denial of climate change appears to mostly be an issue in the United States, where we have the abilities and opportunities to learn and study the evidence that is available; it's particularly advised, I would hope, for those who wish to contribute to changing the course of history here in the US. Politicians accept the responsibility to act in a reasonable manner; denying climate change because it does not fit ones preconceived religious beliefs is unreasonable. What makes this idea much more terrifying is, first, they believe their god is controlling the climate, steering it in a particularly nasty direction; second, they

---

[145] Brian Tashman, "Perkins: There's More Evidence That God Is Behind Natural Disasters Than There Is For Climate Change," http://www.rightwingwatch.org/content/perkins-theres-more-evidence-god-behind-natural-disasters-there-climate-change (February 19, 2014)

wish for this to be true and are quite alright with allowing it to occur because their god said so. We do not need thinking such as this, particularly in secular nations.

Scientology

Scientology has had its share of scandals. From kidnapping to blackmailing, leaders within the movement have made it well known they are immoral, greedy, and dishonest. To top it all off I find the organization to be absolutely fascinating, and not in a "good" sort of way. Their core beliefs are as crazy and strange as most of today's religions, but they're so obviously false it is hard to comprehend how anyone can come to believe the fantasy that L. Ron Hubbard created.

Scientology is a complex cult but their beliefs are easy to hammer down. Sprouted from the imagination of Hubbard, the religion plays out like one of his many science-fiction novels. Scientologists believe we are wretched beings, born with a special presence within us; this presence is what is known as a thetan. To better explain it, this spiritual being is so well intertwined that it's often said we are the thetan, and the thetan is us. The website "What is Scientology?" states:

"An immortal spiritual being; the human soul. The term soul is not used because it has developed so many other meanings from use in other religions and practices that it doesn't describe precisely what was discovered in Scientology. We use the term thetan instead, from the Greek letter theta (Theta), the traditional symbol for thought or life. One does not have a thetan, something one keeps somewhere apart from oneself; one is a thetan. The thetan is the person himself, not his body or his name or the physical universe, his mind or anything else. It is that which is aware of being aware; the identity which IS the individual."[146]

Since we have, and apparently are, thetans, those thetans can then become corrupt with negative energy. The process known as "auditing" can help alleviate that burden. Auditors use what is called an e-meter, or electropsychometer, to determine what the person needs to work through in order to rid the thetan of negativity, which is called "clear." According to the aforementioned website, "clear" is:

"A highly desirable state for the individual, achieved through auditing, which was never attainable before Dianetics. A Clear is a person who no longer has his own reactive mind and therefore suffers none of the ill effects that the reactive mind can cause."[147]

Those who are working to achieve the clear state are considered operating thetans. What truly interests me the most is the machine in which auditors use to pick up disturbances. Did I happen to mention thetans are passed from one human to the next? That being said, the operating thetan of today can be affected by the previous life of the thetan of yesterday. Though the e-meter doesn't seem to possess the powers to detect

[146] "Thetan,"
http://www.whatisscientology.org/html/Part14/Chp50/pg1024-a.html
[147] "Clear," http://www.whatisscientology.org/html/Part14/Chp50/pg1019-a.html

issues regarding thetans, since thetans do not exist, what does it register then?

When an auditor asks a question, the operating thetan will answer. If there is a spike on the e-meter, that question is of a particular importance; it could signify an important event in a past life, or of the current life. This is because the mental anguish is being purged from the thetan as they tell the auditor their deepest and darkest secrets. This makes complete sense, doesn't it? Considering the type of device the e-meter is, of course not. It simply reads electromagnetic waves and as we spill our guts to someone about a shameful occurrence, we as humans do not suddenly expel electromagnetic waves. Terrible science, once again, used to support an unprofessional means of therapy.

Scientology is really only therapy to those who are not "clear". Once an individual becomes so well audited, they no longer trip the e-meter during auditing sessions. Once you work your way through the program, you learn more, bit by bit, about the organization itself; oh, for a little price as well. As an operating thetan, there are levels one travels. In operating thetan level III, or OT III, one learns the creation story of the thetan inside every human being.

Apparently, there was once a man named Xenu, and he was in charge of the Galactic Federation roughly 75 million years ago. As a powerful man, he had to deal with an array of problems; overpopulation being one of them. Because of this, he gathered billions of people and froze them in pods. They were then flown, in apparently spacecraft similar to a DC-8, and dropped around volcanoes all throughout the planet. In order to do these beings in, hydrogen bombs were then dropped into the volcanoes and detonated simultaneously, killing the innocent people. From these people came the thetans, those pesky spirits I've been going on about.

This is, simply stated, nothing but a fantasy story; yet, people still believe it and that disturbs me greatly. I don't necessarily care if someone believes these things to be true; that's not to say I agree with their intent. We are not born wicked, our species was not invaded by alien spirits, and the term "clear" is only found in the crazy annals of Scientology's history. They present themselves as an alternative to evidence-based psychiatric care and that is their greatest error. Taking advantage of those who are weak and vulnerable is reprehensible, and gladly accepting their hard-earned money in exchange for their sanity is as well. One cannot replace the centuries of medicine predating the existence of Scientology and no matter how hard one tries, Scientology will never solve anything; it only creates more problems. While the number of adherents are low in comparison to the three monotheistic religions of today, what they are doing is just as wretched and false as the rest of them.

Summary

Some have said science is a religion altogether, with dogmatic scripture and narrow focus; essentially promoting an atheist worldview. One might believe this to be true because their religion has been outdated, and for good reason. Religion and science have clashed for centuries and, presumably, will continue to until unreasonable ideas and the suppression of information worldwide is thwarted. Galileo Galilei was condemned by the Catholic Church in 1633 because his ideas regarding heliocentrism were considered heresy. After his trial, he was convicted and sentenced to house arrest, where he remained until he died.

This happened for one reason and one reason only: It conflicted with the teachings of the religious body in power. When religious beliefs are left unchallenged, this sometimes happens. Today, in civilized nations, we rarely see such sanctimonious behavior from the pulpits but the tyranny comes not from the pulpits anymore; we see it from the common population and from various levels of government. We shouldn't be afraid to question all things, no matter how many people attempt to kill such an approach. People will continue to defy science and medicine as long as we allow them to. Introduce reason whenever given the opportunity, for we are in dire need of it. Freedom is what we should demand from these organizations and the individuals responsible for maintaining them.

CHAPTER SIX
EQUALITY FOR ALL

A human is a human, and love is love no matter the gender; both are facts. We cherish those who we love and nothing ought to interfere with experiencing the emotions we feel. As a secular humanist, I see no differences between a straight person, a gay person, a lesbian person, a trans-person, and bisexual person. We're all humans, deserving of simple respect and acceptance. Religion, on the other hand, seeks to divide humanity in many distinct ways, one of which is the difference between a straight person and a homosexual person.

Religious beliefs have contributed to the ridicule and persecution of those belonging to the LGBTQI community for hundreds of years, only because they are different from the larger population. Still today many are killed for simply acting on the urges they were born with. It's in great error to condemn someone for things of which they are not in control of. Prominent religious beliefs still continue to interfere with the lives of so many individuals for such silly reasons. Yes, it is silly to mock, ridicule, persecute, and murder someone for being who they are. Religion and faith, quite proudly, stand in the way of personal expression for those who are part of the LGBTQI community. For that reason, the institutions that support homosexual bigotry ought to be a thing of the past; sadly, their presences are felt all around the world because for those who believe, faith is more important than the rights and respect of other individuals.

Treatment of Homosexuals in Scripture

Christians, who believe homosexuals are less than human, often cite various pieces of scripture to bolster their bigoted ideas. Wishing to subjugate homosexuals, they seek the words of their god in order to do so. The label "sodomite" is often given to homosexuals because they represent, to some Christians, the evil people living in the city of Sodom, which was destroyed by God. I wrote earlier about how Lot immorally offered his daughters to the town's people so that God's angels would be spared. Genesis says:

"But before they lay down, the men of the city, even the men of Sodom, compassed the house round, both old and young, all the people from every quarter: And they called unto Lot, and said unto him, where are the men which came in to thee this night? Bring them out unto us, that we may know them."[148]

"Know" is commonly considered to mean rape. So with that, some Christians are equating the rapists of Sodom with the general homosexual population when they call them "sodomites." To that I say, what a disgusting and immoral idea; another attempt to publicly vilify someone because they perceive them as the enemy of God.

---

[148] Genesis 19:4-5 KJV

In Leviticus, God gives commandments and punishments in regards to homosexuals and the practice of sex between those who are. In Leviticus, it is written:

"Thou shalt not lie with mankind, as with womankind: it is abomination."[149]

"If a man also lie with mankind, as he lieth with a woman, both of them have committed an abomination: they shall surely be put to death; their blood shall be upon them."[150]

It's commonly understood that homosexual humans are born with the aforementioned sexual desires. God commands the Jewish people to kill them, apparently because of the way in which they were created by him? This is often why it is hard to understand those who revere such an immoral character as this.

Paul, in the New Testament, brings up homosexuality first in the book of Romans. It is written:

"For this cause God gave them up unto vile affections: for even their women did change the natural use into that which is against nature. And likewise also the men, leaving the natural use of the woman, burned in their lust one toward another; men with men working that which is unseemly, and receiving in themselves that recompense of their error which was meet. And even as they did not like to retain God in their knowledge, God gave them over to a reprobate mind, to do those things which are not convenient"[151]

---

[149] Leviticus 18:22 KJV
[150] Leviticus 20:13 KJV
[151] Romans 1:26-28 KJV

Homosexuality is unnatural? According to Arash Fereydooni of the Yale Scientific:

"Currently, homosexual behavior has been documented in over 450 different animal species worldwide."[152]

In light of the previous statement, homosexuality seems rather natural to me, as it does to all biologists and naturalists. Paul lived during a time when in which little was known about the natural world, so it is to no one's surprise he held these strange beliefs. It's terrible, however, that modern human beings follow such text, often to a tee.

In 1 Corinthians, Paul writes about those who will not be allowed to enter heaven. It is written:

"Know ye not that the unrighteous shall not inherit the kingdom of God? Be not deceived: neither fornicators, nor idolaters, nor adulterers, nor effeminate, nor abusers of themselves with mankind, nor thieves, nor covetous, nor drunkards, nor revilers, nor extortioners, shall inherit the kingdom of God."[153]

"Abusers of themselves with mankind" refers to those who are homosexuals. Again, homosexuals are considered an abnormality; an idea that can also be found in the Koran.

The Koran speaks against homosexuality in a similar fashion. Lot is referenced in the Koran as well, reasserting the claim that homosexuals are sinful be-

---

[152] Arash Fereydooni, "Do Animals Exhibit Homosexuality?"
http://www.yalescientific.org/2012/03/do-animals-exhibit-homosexuality/
(March 14, 2012)
[153] 1 Corinthians 6:9-10 KJV

ings; many of the circumstances in the Koran differ from the Old Testament, but the story is similar enough to draw that conclusion. It is written:

"And Lot! (Remember) when he said unto his folk: Will ye commit abomination such as no creature ever did before you? Lo! ye come with lust unto men instead of women. Nay, but ye are wanton folk."[154]

It is again condemned later in the Koran, where it states:

"What! Of all creatures do ye come unto the males, and leave the wives your Lord created for you ? Nay, but ye are forward folk."[155]

Though the Koran does not explicitly command Muslims to specifically kill those who are homosexual, it still terribly portrays who human beings are as a species. Both of these books, of which are often said to be a gateway to absolute truth, perhaps give the worst prescriptions to follow; that is, if one wishes to live in a rational society.

In Modern Islam

Oppression of the members of the LGBTQI community is most often spawned from religious doctrine; in today's world, most of it comes directly from Christian, Judaic, and Islamic teachings. Free of reason and compassion, Islam is often guilty of some of the most brutal and unreasonable punishments for a crime that

---

[154] Koran 7:80-81
[155] Koran 26:165-166

shouldn't exist. In accordance with the teachings of the Koran, those who belong to the LGBTQI community are subjected to brutality in many of the Islamic theocracies throughout the Middle East and Africa. This, of course, does not mean I categorize every Muslim in this way. Most Muslims are quite progressive; whose moral compasses far surpass the teachings of Muhammad. It is those who act on their faith, which bring about violent behavior, and the very doctrines from which they seek divine inspiration.

Homosexuality and transgender and transsexual behavior is strictly prohibited in Islam and if one is found guilty of these, they may face the death penalty. In order to condemn someone to death in Islam, they must first be deemed as a threat to the teachings of Muhammad. In the Koran, it states:

"Say, 'Come, I will recite what your Lord has prohibited to you. [He commands] that you not associate anything with Him, and to parents, good treatment, and do not kill your children out of poverty; We will provide for you and them. And do not approach immoralities - what is apparent of them and what is concealed. And do not kill the soul which Allah has forbidden [to be killed] except by [legal] right. This has He instructed you that you may use reason.'"[156]

In other words, anyone is free to kill anyone just so long as the person doing the killing can find enough reason by way of their previous religious beliefs. According to the website "About Religion," it contends:

"Islamic philosophy holds that a harsh punishment serves as a deterrent to serious crimes that harm indi-

---

[156] Koran 6:151

vidual victims, or threaten to destabilize the foundation of society."[157]

Individuals are condemned to death for threatening to disturb the fabric of Islam; this is called "Fasad filardh." As a result of this sort of reasoning, hundreds are killed for simply being who they were born as. Any society that wishes to strictly follow the teachings of ancient men and women will always do as those individuals do; this is why, if we wish to live in a reasonable and prosperous society, religion and its influence on the actions of the believer must be extinguished. I've stated on many occasions, of which I'm not afraid to repeat again, I do not wish to rid the world of religion; I do wish to strip it of its privilege.

Without this privilege, countries like Saudi Arabia, Iran, Iraq, and Yemen wouldn't put homosexuals to death. In Yemen, men who are married to women may face harsh punishments if they're found guilty of homosexuality. These result from a code of law passed in 1994, which state:

"Any act that falls on the body of the human being and defames the honor thereof; is carried out from one person to another other than adultery, homosexuality or lesbianism is considered a disgrace to honor"[158]

"Homosexuality is the contact of one man to another through his posterior; both sodomites whether males or females are punished with whipping of one hun-

---

[157] "Capital Punishment in Islam," About Religion, http://islam.about.com/cs/law/a/c_punishment.htm
[158] "Republican Decree for Law No 12 for the Year 1994, Concerning Crimes and Penalties," http://www.ilo.org/dyn/natlex/docs/ELECTRONIC/83557/92354/F15496058 60/YEM83557.pdf

dred strokes if not married. It is admissible to reprimand it by imprisonment for a period not exceeding one year punishment by stoning to death if married."[159]

It is absolutely appalling and disgusting to know that such instances of inhumanity still exist today. Similar laws like this exist in the aforementioned countries; countries that which draw inspiration from the holy word of the Koran. It's unsurprising these countries are among the top 10 countries guilty of executing the most criminals.[160]

In some situations, the death sentence is off the table; they're simply flogged and publicly shamed for being part of the LGBTQI community. For instance, in Saudi Arabia, a country very often committing violent acts against humanity, it is illegal to publicly identify as a member of this community; even going so far as to outlaw sex change operations for that very reason. This could also be because those who enacted the law are unfamiliar with the distinction between those who are transgender and those who are homosexual. It's not uncommon for religious individuals to defy sex change operations; according to their ideas, changing the nature of one's body stands against the nature God created.

If we cannot rise above this sort of tyranny, we will continue to see horror such as this all throughout the world. These sorts of acts, inspired by Islamic

---

[159] "Republican Decree for Law No 12 for the Year 1994, Concerning Crimes and Penalties,"
http://www.ilo.org/dyn/natlex/docs/ELECTRONIC/83557/92354/F15496058 60/YEM83557.pdf
[160] Richard Johnson, "The Death Penality,"
https://nationalpostnews.files.wordpress.com/2012/04/na0428_deathpenalt y.pdf

teachings, happen all around the world, carried out not only by judicial bodies but by individuals whose ideas align with those who wish to keep society in the past. Religion only serves to bolster a false idea, from which barbarous individuals can draw inspiration from. I'm certain we can move along from this stupidity and accept anyone and everyone with loving arms; that is only if we can come together, embrace education and acceptance, and vigorously defend those who have been marginalized for things they have no control over.

In Modern Christianity

As I discussed in a previous chapter, Christianity has done its fair share of damage all throughout history. Today, I contend, the most prevalent bigotry is directed towards those who within the LGBTQI community. Most consider the United States to be quite progressive on social issues, but anti-LGBTQI bigotry still runs rampant throughout the minds of its citizens. In 2014, a Gallup poll:

"...found that 58% of Americans felt gay and lesbian relations were morally acceptable. But Americans' personal opinions about homosexuality do not dictate whether they are satisfied with the current level of acceptance toward it. In a follow-up question that probed Americans who are dissatisfied with the current acceptance of gays for their position, 16% of Americans indicate they want to see more acceptance while 14% want less. Another 10% are dissatisfied, but don't have a preference for whether there should be more or less acceptance."[161]

I can only imagine why the numbers are so low for those who wish for the acceptance of homosexuality; and that's just homosexuality, not considering those who are transgender. With the anti-LGBTQI rhetoric strewn about from the pulpits of American churches, it's terribly hard to fight against the voices that are incredibly loud and undeservingly supported by the general public.

From politicians to preachers, these individuals, who clearly do not understand the extent of human sexuality and human identification, still persistantly believe that heterosexuality is all that exists, men and women were created to be exactly that, and marriage is that which God has ordered, between one man and one woman. On these issues, Christianity has gotten it wrong, right from the beginning. According to the most vocal, however, they believe they are right and their bigotry continues to show.

Michelle Bachmann said in 2004:

"If you're involved in the gay and lesbian lifestyle, it's bondage. It is personal bondage, personal despair and personal enslavement."[162]

[161] "Satisfaction With Acceptance of Gay People Plateaus at 53%," Gallup, http://www.gallup.com/poll/181235/satisfaction-acceptance-gay-people-plat-eaus.aspx?utm_source=homosexuality&utm_medium=search&utm_campaign=tiles

[162] Kate Sheppard, "Bachmann Camp Offers More Questionable Slavery Claims," http://www.motherjones.com/mojo/2011/07/bachmann-camp-offers-more-questionable-slavery-claims (July 11, 2011)

During an interview with the Associated Press, Rick Santorum said:

"Every society in the history of man has upheld the institution of marriage as a bond between a man and a woman. Why? Because society is based on one thing: that society is based on the future of the society. And that's what? Children. Monogamous relationships. In every society, the definition of marriage has not ever to my knowledge included homosexuality. That's not to pick on homosexuality. It's not, you know, man on child, man on dog, or whatever the case may be."

Man on child? Man on dog? When someone equates homosexuality with bestiality and pedophilia, it tells you where they're more than likely coming from ideologically. These are things we often hear as "abominations" according to the religious. To the atheist and skeptic, they're false analogies.

    Religious pundits haven't stayed quiet on this matter either. Pat Robertson, on his television show *The 700 Club,* had this to say:

"You know those who are homosexual will die out because they don't reproduce. You have to have heterosexual sex to reproduce. Same thing with that church. It's doomed. It's going to die out, 'cause it's the most nonsensical thing I have heard in a long time. This is absurd. God has made us to be in families. God has created a desire of men and women to have attraction to the opposite sex so that they will reproduce and have children."[163]

---

[163] Ed Mazza, "Pat Robertson Says Gays 'Will Die Out'," http://www.huffingtonpost.com/2014/12/18/pat-robertson-gays-die-out_n_6345454.html (December 18, 2014)

Pastor John Hagee said in 2013:

"The Bible requirements for getting married are these: One, that you marry someone of the opposite sex....Anything else is two disturbed people playing house."[164]

I once belonged to the Missouri Synod Lutheran Church who held the same views regarding the acceptance of homosexuals.

According to their website, they strictly condemn homosexuality and actively teach against it, while also instructing those within the church to help others out of their homosexual behavior.[165] The Catholic Church also has a similar stance. According to the United States Conference of Catholic Bishops, they believe people with an inclination to homosexuality need ministered to. Their website states:

"The Church seeks to enable every person to live out the universal call to holiness. Persons with a homosexual inclination ought to receive every aid and encouragement to embrace this call personally and fully. This will unavoidably involve much struggle and self-mastery, for following Jesus always means following the way of the Cross..."[166]

---

[164] David Edwards, "Pastor Hagee: Same sex marriage 'is two disturbed people playing house'," http://www.rawstory.com/2013/01/pastor-hagee-same-sex-marriage-is-two-disturbed-people-playing-house/ (January 9, 2013)

[165] Lutheran Church, Missouri Synod, http://www.lcms.org/faqs/lcmsviews#homosexuality

[166] "Homosexuality," United States Conference of Catholic Bishops, http://www.usccb.org/issues-and-action/human-life-and-dignity/homosexuality/ (2006)

The American Baptist Churches USA website shares a similar statement:

"Who submit to the teaching of Scripture that God's design for sexual intimacy places it within the context of marriage between one man and one woman, and acknowledge that the practice of homosexuality is incompatible with Biblical teaching."[167]

It's quite rare to find a Christian organization that upholds homosexuality. You'll find acceptance of homosexuals, anyone in the LGBTQI community for that matter, in most non-denominational churches. Though small in number, they challenge the very book they cling to.

I truly think they're the only ones catching on and changing with the times; reminiscent of the Mormon Church and their flop on allowing non-Caucasians to hold priesthood, which God just so happened to change his mind on when the United States raged during the Civil Rights movement of the 1960's.

In other parts of the world, Catholicism essentially dominates the landscape, hold the world in its vile and archaic clutches. Countries in Africa suffer from the influence of fundamental Christian ideas, often said to be a result of mission work coming from the United States. For instance, in 2014 Uganda passed a bill strictly prohibiting homosexual behavior, which also gave the countries judicial body to strictly punish those found guilty thereof. All of the violations within the bill are absolutely ridiculous, harboring equally ridiculous punishments. According to the bill, almost

---

[167] "Identity Statement," American Baptist Churches USA, http://www.abc-usa.org/about-us/identity-statement-2005/ (2005)

137

everything in relation to homosexuality, even distributing pro-homosexual rights material, is absolutely illegal; the country essentially treats homosexuality as it would any other sexually aggravated crime.[168]

The Christian denominations that strictly condemn homosexuality and transgenderism are perhaps the most adherent in regards to what the Bible says on the matter. They believe their god disapproves and they're completely correct according to the book they sheepishly follow; never mind the fact that most wear clothing with two different types of fabrics and dine on shell fish. What they fail to realize could prove quite important for those who find themselves stuck in a situation they cannot leave. People are people, sexuality is complex, and a god has nothing to do with someone's sexual disposition. However, let's not wait for Christianity to catch up with the rational world. It's time we leave them in our dust.

The Fight for Gay Marriage in the United States

As I'm writing his portion, the Supreme Court of the United States is hearing testimony as to whether or not it is unconstitutional to deny gay and lesbian couples the right to marry in all fifty states. As of right now, 37 states currently allow gay marriage, as that particular form of legislation is left for the state to decide. 26 of the states which allow gay marriage achieved this goal through private state court decisions. Even in some states, same-sex couples can obtain a county marriage license but the state will not

---

[168] The Anti-Homosexuality Act, 2014,"
http://wp.patheos.com.s3.amazonaws.com/blogs/warrenthrockmorton/files/2014/02/Anti-Homosexuality-Act-2014.pdf

recognize the union. It's been a long and arduous battle, but it's a battle worth fighting none the less.

This is not about whether we let the religious win; it's about whether or not love prevails. Love is all this has been about. A heterosexual couple can love and feel pain the same as a gay couple. We're all human beings, and as long as the country recognizes one, it must recognize the other. Marriage isn't strictly about creating children or unifying a bond with any god. It's about forming a union with another individual; a union that means something different to every individual. Not a single religious ideology should stand in the way of that. Yet, on every single occasion it's given the opportunity, it has.

For most of its past, the United States did not legally recognize same-sex marriages. However, the subject was eventually challenged because most states did not explicitly deny the right to marry; few states held legislation particularly banning same-sex couples. In 2004, Massachusetts became the first state to legally recognize gay marriage. Before the passing, only 4 states restricted marriage to a single man and a single woman. Afterward, between 2004 and 2013, 14 states passed legislation denying same sex couples the right to marry.

During that period of time, some improvements were made. Eleven states passed laws allowing same-sex couples to marry. Perhaps the most well-known and heated battle was that between civil rights supporters and Proposition 8 in California. During the 2008 elections, Californian voters had the opportunity to kill an amendment that would prohibit same-sex couples from the right to marry. The amendment simply stated:

"Only marriage between a man and a woman is valid or recognized in California."[169]

It was vigorously challenged all throughout California, but if it wasn't for the massive amount of money, supplied by Mormon millionaires, it wouldn't have passed. Even many politicians supported the amendment; John McCain said in support:

"I support the efforts of the people of California to recognize marriage as a unique institution between a man and a woman, just as we did in my home state of Arizona. I do not believe judges should be making these decisions."[170]

Mitt Romney even donated $10,000 to the Proposition 8 campaign.[171] Along with political support, over ten religious organizations in California supported the amendment. Sadly, it was enough to push the bill through. This wasn't the end of the fight, however. Same-sex marriage supporters continued to fight the ban, taking the case to the California Supreme Court. A set-back hit when the California Supreme Court upheld the passing of Proposition 8, but eventually DOMA, the Defense of Marriage Act, was ruled unconstitutional by a United States District Court under similar set of circumstances.

---

169 "Text of Proposed Laws,"
http://www.voterguide.sos.ca.gov/past/2008/general/text-proposed-laws/text-of-proposed-laws.pdf
170 Justin Ewers, "McCain Supports Efforts to Ban Gay Marriage,"
http://www.usnews.com/news/campaign-2008/articles/2008/06/27/mccain-supports-efforts-to-ban-gay-marriage (June 27, 2008)
171 Scottie Tompston, "Mitt Romney donated $10,000 to NOM to help pass Proposition 8," http://www.equalityontrial.com/2012/03/30/mitt-romney-donated-10000-to-nom-to-help-pass-proposition-8/ (March 30, 2012)

With that, the fight was back on. During a new trial, the plaintiffs argued:

"'Proposition 8 places the force of law behind stigmas against gays and lesbians, including: gays and lesbians do not have intimate relationships similar to heterosexual couples; gays and lesbians are not as good as heterosexuals; and gay and lesbian relationships do not deserve the full recognition of society.'"[172]

In this case, the plaintiffs were victorious; same-sex marriage was once again recognized in the state of California. With DOMA being unconstitutional and the fight against Proposition 8 won, similar states would follow suite and defeat previous legislation restricting the right to marry to only different-sex couples.

Arguments were attempted from those who support anti-gay marriage legislation has been resoundingly criticized; a popular one being: developing a suitable environment for child rearing. As one digs further, each and every argument against same-sex marriage come from a religious position, and since the United States is a secular nation, those arguments fall by the wayside. Not a single suitable secular argument against same-sex marriage has been proposed. After 2013, states either passed legislation allowing same-sex marriage or were ordered to do so by federal judges. All states are yet to completely restore civil rights to its people, as they should; I hope, in June, the

---

172 Andy Eddins, "Prop 8 overturned: Freedom to marry ban struck down in California," http://www.freedomtomarry.org/blog/entry/prop-8-overturned-freedom-to-marry-ban-struck-down-in-california (August 8, 2010)

justices, part of the Supreme Court of the United States, feel the exact same way.

Conversion Therapy

Conversion therapy is almost all around supported by prominent Christian leaders and the organizations they represent. Conversion therapy is specifically designed to influence gay, lesbian, and transgender individuals to live a life of strict heterosexuality. Most often, the organizations that offer this type of service tend to do so in a religious way, influencing the individual to fight their inborn urges in order to follow the teachings of the Bible.

This, as I stated previously, is very telling; not a single bit of evidence supports the idea that homosexuality and transgenderism are things that which can be changed by shear will. These individuals are born this way, leaving one to speculate as to whether conversion therapy organizations are doing more harm than good; I am willing to say they are gravely mistaken in their ideology. The American Psychological Association also believes so, stating on their website:

"All major national mental health organizations have officially expressed concerns about therapies promoted to modify sexual orientation. To date, there has been no scientifically adequate research to show that therapy aimed at changing sexual orientation (sometimes called reparative or conversion therapy) is safe or effective. Furthermore, it seems likely that the promotion of change therapies reinforces stereotypes and contributes to a negative climate for lesbian, gay and bisexual persons."[173]

It's incredibly hard for me to understand the amount of stress religious doctrine places on those who have to live as though they're in constant sin. As an atheist, I clearly do not follow a mistaken doctrine. The religious, as wrong as they may be, feel as though they are clearly on the right side of the argument. That being said, their failings to understand human sexuality keeps them from reaching a reasonable conclusion; their religiously-inspired misunderstandings create a negative environment for those who wish to live their lives as they should.

Therapy sessions focus primarily on indoctrinating the patient with religious pronouncements, leaving them feeling guilty for upsetting their god. Sometimes, session leaders will dive into the patients past, believing some traumatic incident is to blame for their "sexual rebellion." It's often said gay and lesbian individuals are as they are because they experienced sexual abuse as a child. This is a grossly inaccurate and utterly disgusting assertion, of which holds no weight. In other situations, gay men are sometimes prescribed estrogen to reduce their libido. Deservingly, conversion therapy organizations are catching heat from activists and politicians.

Recently, President Barack Obama supported the banning of conversion therapy for those under the age of 18. This response was brought about by a White House petition calling for the ban, titled, "Leelah's Law." The bill's name was inspired by Leelah Alcorn,

---

[173] "What about therapy intended to change sexual orientation from gay to straight?," American Psychological Association, http://www.apa.org/topics/LGBTQI/orientation.aspx

a young transgender woman who committed suicide. She did not experience acceptance from her family, particularly her mother and father, who attempted to use conversion therapy; this event, along with a number of other instances of bullying, created tragedy. In her suicide note, Leelah wrote:

"My mom started taking me to a therapist, but would only take me to Christian therapists, (who were all very biased) so I never actually got the therapy I needed to cure me of my depression. I only got more Christians telling me that I was selfish and wrong and that I should look to God for help."[174]

Later in the note, she wrote:

"Either I live the rest of my life as a lonely man who wishes he were a woman or I live my life as a lonelier woman who hates herself. There's no winning. There's no way out. I'm sad enough already, I don't need my life to get any worse."[175]

I was terribly saddened upon reading about this poor woman. She did not deserve this type of treatment; no one in the LGBTQI community deserves this kind of treatment. They are human beings and nothing less than that. There isn't something wrong with them; they aren't broken or sick or in need of divine salvation. The only salvation they are in need of is from the torment and marginalization they receive from those

---

[174] "Suicide Note," https://web.archive.org/web/20150101052635/http://lazerprincess.tumblr.com/post/106447705738/suicide-note
[175] "Suicide Note," https://web.archive.org/web/20150101052635/http://lazerprincess.tumblr.com/post/106447705738/suicide-note

inspired by Christianity. Conversion therapy is on the decline; let us hope this remains the case.

Summary

The religious prejudice against those in the LGBTQI community must come to an end. The excuses given from religious groups and leaders are insufficient compared to the thinking of today. There is no rational reason in which one can use to justify the bigotry gays, lesbians, bisexuals, and transgenders experience on a daily basis. They experience this, in large part, due to the misinformation and hate-speech spread by those who stand in the glory of their god; the calling of their faith from the doctrine of hate it upholds.

Humanism must be first and foremost; this being why some of the religiously-inspired so actively fight against it. It's their job to be the *only* individuals with privilege and status; anyone else who isn't like them is deserving of nothing. This is why I argue against faith and religion so adamantly. Faith seeks to divide, whereas humanism seeks to bring us together. Which do you think deserves the most respect and admiration?

A CHANGE FOR REASON

We need to bring about change if we wish to build a society of critical thinkers and skeptics. Bringing a rise in reason needs to be our top priority, and with that, I believe it will drive away religion until it isn't as strong of a force as it is today. We should be free to exercise our atheism and skepticism without the fear of religious condemnation and social rejection. We should be allowed to question everything. There is absolutely nothing wrong with suspending a belief in something that bears little evidence supporting its existence, and it's completely alright to reject an institution that has stood for nothing but terror, suppression, racism, and the acceptance of unintellectual reasoning.

We need to provide a safe place for our children to grow, to learn, and to self-express. They are our future, and for them we need to make sure we leave a suitable environment to inherit. They absolutely depend on our support, which we must do in a rational and mature way. We must stand against doctrines and ideas that threaten to strangle the flow of knowledge that the young ones are in such desperate need of. We must protect the innocent from the suppressive nature of religion.

We must empower those who the religious have marginalized. They need the support of everyone before we can enact social change in their favor. Women, those in the LGBTQI community, and those of different ethnicities suffer the most in the United States; other countries are fighting similar battles all throughout the world. I'm a young man and I wish to see the acceptance and empowerment of those I previously mentioned before I pass on from this life. We've made great changes in just the past century, but imagine how much more change we can create if we band together and tear down the privilege religious faith has, unfortunately, earned over the course of human history.

We must choose reason over faith in every situation. Critical thinking and reason-based decision making can alleviate the issues I presented throughout this book. Religion and institutionalized superstition does not deserve reverence from the general population. We must find ways to bring awareness to the atheist and skeptic community. We need to inspire activism, whether it's blogging, book writing, picketing, marching, lobbying, or financially supporting those who are more capable and willing to take up the fight to end religious tyranny. Reason is on our minds but we must find a way to make it our policy. I wrote this book to inspire activism, and I hope I have accomplished just that. Faith and its reign of suppression must come to an end. That can happen, only if we embrace love, acceptance, free-thinking, and most of all, reason.

GET INVOLVED

There are numerous ways in which one can become active or find support in atheist and secular communities all around the world. Below, you'll find a list of groups and organizations that can help one either find support or the resources necessary to become active in the aforementioned communities.

Atheist Alliance International, Worldwide, http://www.atheistalliance.org/

International Humanist and Ethical Union, Worldwide, http://www.iheu.org/

American Atheists, United States, https://www.atheists.org/

American Humanist Association, United States, http://www.americanhumanist.org/

Americans United, United States, http://www.au.org/

Center for Inquiry, United States, http://www.centerforinquiry.net/

Freedom from Religion Foundation, United States, http://ffrf.org/
Secular Coalition of America, United States, http://www.secular.org/

Secular Student Alliance, United States,
http://www.secularstudents.org/

Humanist Association of Canada, Canada,
http://www.humanistcanada.com/

Center for Inquiry Canada, Canada,
http://www.cficanada.ca/

British Humanist Society, United Kingdom,
http://www.humanism.org.uk/

Humanist Society Scotland, United Kingdom,
http://www.humanism-scotland.org.uk/

Philippine Atheists and Agnostics Society, Philippines, http://patas.co/

Humanist Society of New Zealand, New Zealand,
http://www.humanist.org.nz/

Humanist Association of Ireland, Ireland,
http://www.humanism.ie/

Indian Rationalist Association, India,
http://www.rationalistinternational.net/

ABOUT THE AUTHOR

J. D. Brucker is an atheist author and blogger, a secular humanist, and an outspoken anti-theist. He is the author of *Improbable: Issues with the God Hypothesis* and *God Needs To Go: Why Christian Beliefs Fail*. Currently, Brucker writes for the *Atheist Republic* and *Patheos* websites. Other works can be found on various secular websites, including *The Richard Dawkins Foundation for Reason and Science* and *The Natural Skeptic*.

Visit his website at: www.jdbrucker.com

Follow on Twitter at: @jdbrucker

CPSIA information can be obtained at www.ICGtesting.com
Printed in the USA
LVOW10s2206200816

501211LV00037B/1127/P